CATHC
SUNDAY
MISSAL
2021 EDITION

Catholic Laity Publishing

Published by Catholic Laity Publishing
473 Burnside Court
Phoenix, Arizona 85040
United States of America

ISBN: 9798502696500

CONTENTS

JANUARY

SOLEMNITY OF MARY, THE MOTHER OF GOD

First Reading: Numbers 6:22-27

The LORD said to Moses: "Speak to Aaron and his sons and tell them: This is how you shall bless the Israelites. Say to them: The LORD bless you and keep you! The LORD let his face shine upon you, and be gracious to you! The LORD look upon you kindly and give you peace! So shall they invoke my name upon the Israelites, and I will bless them."

Responsorial Psalm: Psalm 67:2-3, 5, 6, 8

R. (2a) May God bless us in his mercy.

May God have pity on us and bless us; may he let his face shine upon us. So may your way be known upon earth; among all nations, your salvation. **R.**

May the nations be glad and exult because you rule the peoples in equity; the nations on the earth you guide. **R.**

May the peoples praise you, O God; may all the peoples praise you! May God bless us, and may all the ends of the earth fear him! **R.**

Second Reading: Galatians 4:4-7

1

Brothers and sisters: When the fullness of time had come, God sent his Son, born of a woman, born under the law, to ransom those under the law, so that we might receive adoption as sons. As proof that you are sons, God sent the Spirit of his Son into our hearts, crying out, "Abba, Father!" So you are no longer a slave but a son, and if a son then also an heir, through God.

Alleluia: Hebrews 1:1-2
R. Alleluia, alleluia.
In the past God spoke to our ancestors through the prophets; in these last days, he has spoken to us through the Son. **R.**

Gospel: Luke 2:16-21
The shepherds went in haste to Bethlehem and found Mary and Joseph, and the infant lying in the manger. When they saw this, they made known the message that had been told them about this child. All who heard it were amazed by what had been told them by the shepherds. And Mary kept all these things, reflecting on them in her heart. Then the shepherds returned, glorifying and praising God for all they had heard and seen, just as it had been told to them. When eight days were completed for his circumcision, he was

named Jesus, the name given him by the angel before he was conceived in the womb.

SUNDAY, JANUARY 3
THE EPIPHANY OF THE LORD
First Reading: Isaiah 60:1-6

Rise up in splendor, Jerusalem! Your light has come, the glory of the Lord shines upon you. See, darkness covers the earth, and thick clouds cover the peoples; but upon you the LORD shines, and over you appears his glory. Nations shall walk by your light, and kings by your shining radiance. Raise your eyes and look about; they all gather and come to you: your sons come from afar, and your daughters in the arms of their nurses. Then you shall be radiant at what you see, your heart shall throb and overflow, for the riches of the sea shall be emptied out before you, the wealth of nations shall be brought to you. Caravans of camels shall fill you, dromedaries from Midian and Ephah; all from Sheba shall come bearing gold and frankincense, and proclaiming the praises of the LORD.

Responsorial Psalm: Psalm 72:1-2, 7-8, 10-11, 12-13
R. (11) Lord, every nation on earth will adore you.

O God, with your judgment endow the king, and with your

justice, the king's son; He shall govern your people with justice and your afflicted ones with judgment. **R.**

Justice shall flower in his days, and profound peace, till the moon be no more. May he rule from sea to sea, and from the River to the ends of the earth. **R.**

The kings of Tarshish and the Isles shall offer gifts; the kings of Arabia and Seba shall bring tribute. All kings shall pay him homage, all nations shall serve him. **R.**

For he shall rescue the poor when he cries out, and the afflicted when he has no one to help him. He shall have pity for the lowly and the poor; the lives of the poor he shall save. **R.**

Second Reading: Ephesians 3:2-3a, 5-6

Brothers and sisters: You have heard of the stewardship of God's grace that was given to me for your benefit, namely, that the mystery was made known to me by revelation. It was not made known to people in other generations as it has now been revealed to his holy apostles and prophets by the Spirit: that the Gentiles are coheirs, members of the same body, and copartners in the promise in Christ Jesus through the gospel.

Alleluia: Matthew 2:2

R. Alleluia, alleluia.

We saw his star at its rising and have come to do him homage. **R.**

Gospel: Matthew 2:1-12

When Jesus was born in Bethlehem of Judea, in the days of King Herod, behold, magi from the east arrived in Jerusalem, saying, "Where is the newborn king of the Jews? We saw his star at its rising and have come to do him homage." When King Herod heard this, he was greatly troubled, and all Jerusalem with him. Assembling all the chief priests and the scribes of the people, He inquired of them where the Christ was to be born. They said to him, "In Bethlehem of Judea, for thus it has been written through the prophet: *And you, Bethlehem, land of Judah, are by no means least among the rulers of Judah; since from you shall come a ruler, who is to shepherd my people Israel.*" Then Herod called the magi secretly and ascertained from them the time of the star's appearance. He sent them to Bethlehem and said, "Go and search diligently for the child. When you have found him, bring me word, that I too may go and do him homage." After their audience with the king they set out. And behold, the star that they had seen at its rising preceded them, until it came and stopped over the place where the child was.

They were overjoyed at seeing the star, and on entering the house they saw the child with Mary his mother. They prostrated themselves and did him homage. Then they opened their treasures and offered him gifts of gold, frankincense, and myrrh. And having been warned in a dream not to return to Herod, they departed for their country by another way.

SUNDAY, JANUARY 10
THE BAPTISM OF THE LORD
First Reading: Isaiah 42:1-4, 6-7 or 55:1-11
Isaiah 42:1-4, 6-7

Thus says the LORD: Here is my servant whom I uphold, my chosen one with whom I am pleased, upon whom I have put my spirit; he shall bring forth justice to the nations, not crying out, not shouting, not making his voice heard in the street. A bruised reed he shall not break, and a smoldering wick he shall not quench, until he establishes justice on the earth; the coastlands will wait for his teaching. I, the LORD, have called you for the victory of justice, I have grasped you by the hand; I formed you, and set you as a covenant of the people, a light for the nations, to open the eyes of the blind, to bring out prisoners from confinement, and from the dungeon, those who live in darkness.

Or:

Isaiah 55:1-11

Thus says the LORD: All you who are thirsty, come to the water! You who have no money, come, receive grain and eat; come, without paying and without cost, drink wine and milk! Why spend your money for what is not bread, your wages for what fails to satisfy? Heed me, and you shall eat well, you shall delight in rich fare. Come to me heedfully, listen, that you may have life. I will renew with you the everlasting covenant, the benefits assured to David. As I made him a witness to the peoples, a leader and commander of nations, so shall you summon a nation you knew not, and nations that knew you not shall run to you, because of the LORD, your God, the Holy One of Israel, who has glorified you. Seek the LORD while he may be found, call him while he is near. Let the scoundrel forsake his way, and the wicked man his thoughts; let him turn to the LORD for mercy; to our God, who is generous in forgiving. For my thoughts are not your thoughts, nor are your ways my ways, says the LORD. As high as the heavens are above the earth so high are my ways above your ways and my thoughts above your thoughts. For just as from the heavens the rain and snow come down and do not return there till they have watered the earth, making it fertile and fruitful, giving seed to the one who sows and bread to the one who eats, so shall my word be that goes forth from my mouth; my word shall not return to me void, but shall do my will, achieving the end for which I sent it.

Responsorial Psalm: Psalm 29:1-2, 3-4, 9-10 or Isaiah 12:2-3, 4bcd, 5-6

Psalm 29:1-2, 3-4, 9-10

R (11b) The Lord will bless his people with peace.

Give to the LORD, you sons of God, give to the LORD glory and praise, Give to the LORD the glory due his name; adore the LORD in holy attire. **R.**

The voice of the LORD is over the waters, the LORD, over vast waters. The voice of the LORD is mighty; the voice of the LORD is majestic. **R.**

The God of glory thunders, and in his temple all say, "Glory!" The LORD is enthroned above the flood; the LORD is enthroned as king forever. **R.**

Or:

Isaiah 12:2-3, 4bcd, 5-6

R. (3) You will draw water joyfully from the springs of salvation.

God indeed is my savior; I am confident and unafraid. My

strength and my courage is the LORD, and he has been my savior. With joy you will draw water at the fountain of salvation. **R.**

Give thanks to the LORD, acclaim his name; among the nations make known his deeds, proclaim how exalted is his name. **R.**

Sing praise to the LORD for his glorious achievement; let this be known throughout all the earth. Shout with exultation, O city of Zion, for great in your midst is the Holy One of Israel! **R.**

Second Reading: Acts 10:34-38 or 1 John 5:1-9
Acts 10:34-38

Peter proceeded to speak to those gathered in the house of Cornelius, saying: "In truth, I see that God shows no partiality. Rather, in every nation whoever fears him and acts uprightly is acceptable to him. You know the word that he sent to the Israelites as he proclaimed peace through Jesus Christ, who is Lord of all, what has happened all over Judea, beginning in Galilee after the baptism that John preached, how God anointed Jesus of Nazareth with the Holy Spirit and power. He went about doing good and healing all those oppressed by the devil, for God was with him."

Or:

1 John 5:1-9

Beloved: Everyone who believes that Jesus is the Christ is begotten by God, and everyone who loves the Father loves also the one begotten by him. In this way we know that we love the children of God when we love God and obey his commandments. For the love of God is this, that we keep his commandments. And his commandments are not burdensome, for whoever is begotten by God conquers the world. And the victory that conquers the world is our faith. Who indeed is the victor over the world but the one who believes that Jesus is the Son of God? This is the one who came through water and blood, Jesus Christ, not by water alone, but by water and blood. The Spirit is the one who testifies, and the Spirit is truth. So there are three that testify, the Spirit, the water, and the blood, and the three are of one accord. If we accept human testimony, the testimony of God is surely greater. Now the testimony of God is this, that he has testified on behalf of his Son.

Alleluia: John 1:29

R. Alleluia, alleluia.

John saw Jesus approaching him, and said: Behold the Lamb

of God who takes away the sin of the world. **R.**

Gospel: Mark 1:7-11

This is what John the Baptist proclaimed: "One mightier than I is coming after me. I am not worthy to stoop and loosen the thongs of his sandals. I have baptized you with water; he will baptize you with the Holy Spirit." It happened in those days that Jesus came from Nazareth of Galilee and was baptized in the Jordan by John. On coming up out of the water he saw the heavens being torn open and the Spirit, like a dove, descending upon him. And a voice came from the heavens, "You are my beloved Son; with you I am well pleased."

SUNDAY, JANUARY 17
SECOND SUNDAY OF ORDINARY TIME
First Reading: 1 Samuel 3:3b-10, 19

Samuel was sleeping in the temple of the LORD where the ark of God was. The LORD called to Samuel, who answered, "Here I am." Samuel ran to Eli and said, "Here I am. You called me." "I did not call you," Eli said. "Go back to sleep." So he went back to sleep. Again the LORD called Samuel, who rose and went to Eli. "Here I am," he said. "You called me." But Eli answered, "I did not call you, my son. Go back to sleep." At that time Samuel was not familiar with the LORD, because the LORD had not revealed anything to him as yet. The LORD called Samuel again, for the third time. Getting up and going to Eli, he said, "Here I am. You called me." Then Eli understood that the LORD was calling the youth. So he said to Samuel, "Go to sleep, and if you are called, reply, Speak, LORD, for your servant is listening." When Samuel went to sleep in his place, the LORD came and revealed his presence, calling out as before, "Samuel, Samuel!" Samuel answered, "Speak, for your servant is listening." Samuel grew up, and the LORD was with him, not permitting any word of his to be without effect.

Responsorial Psalm: Psalm 40:2, 4, 7-8, 8-9, 10
R. (8a and 9a) Here am I, Lord; I come to do your will.
I have waited, waited for the LORD, and he stooped toward me and heard my cry. And he put a new song into my mouth, a hymn to our God. **R.**
Sacrifice or offering you wished not, but ears open to obedience you gave me. Holocausts or sin-offerings you sought not; then said I, "Behold I come." **R.**
"In the written scroll it is prescribed for me, to do your will, O my God, is my delight, and your law is within my heart!" **R.**

I announced your justice in the vast assembly; I did not restrain my lips, as you, O LORD, know. **R.**

Second Reading: 1 Corinthians 6:13c-15a, 17-20

Brothers and sisters: The body is not for immorality, but for the Lord, and the Lord is for the body; God raised the Lord and will also raise us by his power. Do you not know that your bodies are members of Christ? But whoever is joined to the Lord becomes one Spirit with him. Avoid immorality. Every other sin a person commits is outside the body, but the immoral person sins against his own body. Do you not know that your body is a temple of the Holy Spirit within you, whom you have from God, and that you are not your own? For you have been purchased at a price. Therefore glorify God in your body.

Alleluia: John 1:41, 17b
R. Alleluia, alleluia.
We have found the Messiah: Jesus Christ, who brings us truth and grace. **R.**

Gospel: John 1:35-42

John was standing with two of his disciples, and as he watched Jesus walk by, he said, "Behold, the Lamb of God."

The two disciples heard what he said and followed Jesus. Jesus turned and saw them following him and said to them, "What are you looking for?" They said to him, "Rabbi" — which translated means Teacher — "where are you staying?" He said to them, "Come, and you will see." So they went and saw where Jesus was staying, and they stayed with him that day. It was about four in the afternoon. Andrew, the brother of Simon Peter, was one of the two who heard John and followed Jesus. He first found his own brother Simon and told him, "We have found the Messiah" — which is translated Christ. Then he brought him to Jesus. Jesus looked at him and said, "You are Simon the son of John; you will be called Cephas" — which is translated Peter.

SUNDAY, JANUARY 24
THIRD SUNDAY IN ORDINARY TIME
First Reading: Jonah 3:1-5, 10

The word of the LORD came to Jonah, saying: "Set out for the great city of Nineveh, and announce to it the message that I will tell you." So Jonah made ready and went to Nineveh, according to the LORD'S bidding. Now Nineveh was an enormously large city; it took three days to go through it. Jonah began his journey through the city, and had gone but a single day's walk announcing, "Forty days more and Nineveh shall be destroyed," when the people of Nineveh believed God; they proclaimed a fast and all of them, great and small, put on sackcloth. When God saw by their actions how they turned from their evil way, he repented of the evil that he had threatened to do to them; he did not carry it out.

Responsorial Psalm: Psalm 25:4-5, 6-7, 8-9
R. (4a) Teach me your ways, O Lord.
Your ways, O LORD, make known to me; teach me your paths, Guide me in your truth and teach me, for you are God my savior. **R.**
Remember that your compassion, O LORD, and your love are from of old. In your kindness remember me, because of your goodness, O LORD. **R.**
Good and upright is the LORD; thus he shows sinners the way. He guides the humble to justice and teaches the humble his way. **R.**

Second Reading: 1 Corinthians 7:29-31
I tell you, brothers and sisters, the time is running out. From now on, let those having wives act as not having them, those weeping as not weeping, those rejoicing as not rejoicing,

those buying as not owning, those using the world as not using it fully. For the world in its present form is passing away.

Alleluia: Mark 1:15
R. Alleluia, alleluia.
The kingdom of God is at hand. Repent and believe in the Gospel. **R.**

Gospel: Mark 1:14-20
After John had been arrested, Jesus came to Galilee proclaiming the gospel of God: "This is the time of fulfillment. The kingdom of God is at hand. Repent, and believe in the gospel." As he passed by the Sea of Galilee, he saw Simon and his brother Andrew casting their nets into the sea; they were fishermen. Jesus said to them, "Come after me, and I will make you fishers of men." Then they abandoned their nets and followed him. He walked along a little farther and saw James, the son of Zebedee, and his brother John. They too were in a boat mending their nets. Then he called them. So they left their father Zebedee in the boat along with the hired men and followed him.

MONDAY, JANUARY 25
FEAST OF THE CONVERSION OF SAINT PAUL, APOSTLE

First Reading: Acts 22:3-16 or 9:1-22

Acts 22:3-16

Paul addressed the people in these words: "I am a Jew, born in Tarsus in Cilicia, but brought up in this city. At the feet of Gamaliel I was educated strictly in our ancestral law and was zealous for God, just as all of you are today. I persecuted this Way to death, binding both men and women and delivering them to prison. Even the high priest and the whole council of elders can testify on my behalf. For from them I even received letters to the brothers and set out for Damascus to bring back to Jerusalem in chains for punishment those there as well. "On that journey as I drew near to Damascus, about noon a great light from the sky suddenly shone around me. I fell to the ground and heard a voice saying to me, 'Saul, Saul, why are you persecuting me?' I replied, 'Who are you, sir?' And he said to me, 'I am Jesus the Nazorean whom you are persecuting.' My companions saw the light but did not hear the voice of the one who spoke to me. I asked, 'What shall I do, sir?' The Lord answered me, 'Get up and go into Damascus, and there you will be told about everything appointed for you to do.'

Since I could see nothing because of the brightness of that light, I was led by hand by my companions and entered Damascus. "A certain Ananias, a devout observer of the law, and highly spoken of by all the Jews who lived there, came to me and stood there and said, 'Saul, my brother, regain your sight.' And at that very moment I regained my sight and saw him. Then he said, 'The God of our ancestors designated you to know his will, to see the Righteous One, and to hear the sound of his voice; for you will be his witness before all to what you have seen and heard. Now, why delay? Get up and have yourself baptized and your sins washed away, calling upon his name.'"

Or:

Acts 9:1-22

Saul, still breathing murderous threats against the disciples of the Lord, went to the high priest and asked him for letters to the synagogues in Damascus, that, if he should find any men or women who belonged to the Way, he might bring them back to Jerusalem in chains. On his journey, as he was nearing Damascus, a light from the sky suddenly flashed around him. He fell to the ground and heard a voice saying to him, "Saul, Saul, why are you persecuting me?" He said, "Who are you, sir?" The reply came, "I am Jesus, whom you are persecuting. Now get up and go into the city and you will be told what you must do." The men who were traveling with him stood speechless, for they heard the voice but could see no one. Saul got up from the ground, but when he opened his eyes he could see nothing; so they led him by the hand and brought him to Damascus. For three days he was unable to see, and he neither ate nor drank. There was a disciple in Damascus named Ananias, and the Lord said to him in a vision, Ananias." He answered, "Here I am, Lord." The Lord said to him, "Get up and go to the street called Straight and ask at the house of Judas for a man from Tarsus named Saul. He is there praying, and in a vision he has seen a man named Ananias come in and lay his hands on him, that he may regain his sight." But Ananias replied, "Lord, I have heard from many sources about this man, what evil things he has done to your holy ones in Jerusalem. And here he has authority from the chief priests to imprison all who call upon your name." But the Lord said to him, "Go, for this man is a chosen instrument of mine to carry my name before Gentiles, kings, and children of Israel, and I will show him what he will have to suffer for my name." So Ananias went and entered the house; laying his hands on him, he said, "Saul, my brother, the Lord has sent me, Jesus who appeared to you on the way by which you came, that you may regain your sight and be filled with the Holy Spirit." Immediately things like scales fell from his eyes and he regained his sight. He got up and was baptized, and when he had eaten, he recovered his strength. He stayed some days with the disciples in Damascus, and he began at once to proclaim Jesus in the synagogues, that he is the Son of God. All who heard him were astounded and said, "Is not this the man who in Jerusalem ravaged those who call upon this name, and came here expressly to take them back in chains to the chief priests?" But Saul grew all the stronger and confounded the Jews who lived in Damascus, proving that this is the Christ.

Responsorial Psalm: Psalm 117:1bc, 2
R. (Mark 16:15) Go out to all the world, and tell the Good News.
Or:
R. Alleluia, alleluia.
Praise the LORD, all you nations; glorify him, all you peoples! **R.**
For steadfast is his kindness toward us, and the fidelity of the Lord endures forever. **R.**

Alleluia: John 15:16

R. Alleluia, alleluia.

I chose you from the world, to go and bear fruit that will last, says the Lord. **R.**

Gospel: Mark 16:15-18

Jesus appeared to the Eleven and said to them: "Go into the whole world and proclaim the Gospel to every creature. Whoever believes and is baptized will be saved; whoever does not believe will be condemned. These signs will accompany those who believe: in my name they will drive out demons, they will speak new languages. They will pick up serpents with their hands, and if they drink any deadly thing, it will not harm them. They will lay hands on the sick, and they will recover."

SUNDAY, JANUARY 31

FOURTH SUNDAY IN ORDINARY TIME

First Reading: Deuteronomy 18:15-20

Moses spoke to all the people, saying: "A prophet like me will the LORD, your God, raise up for you from among your own kin; to him you shall listen. This is exactly what you requested of the LORD, your God, at Horeb on the day of the assembly, when you said, 'Let us not again hear the voice of the LORD, our God, nor see this great fire any more, lest we die.' And the LORD said to me, 'This was well said. I will raise up for them a prophet like you from among their kin, and will put my words into his mouth; he shall tell them all that I command him. Whoever will not listen to my words which he speaks in my name, I myself will make him answer for it. But if a prophet presumes to speak in my name an oracle that I have not commanded him to speak, or speaks in the name of other gods, he shall die.'"

Responsorial Psalm: Psalm 95:1-2, 6-7, 7-9
R. (8) If today you hear his voice, harden not your hearts.
Come, let us sing joyfully to the LORD; let us acclaim the rock of our salvation. Let us come into his presence with thanksgiving; let us joyfully sing psalms to him. **R.**
Come, let us bow down in worship; let us kneel before the LORD who made us. For he is our God, and we are the people he shepherds, the flock he guides. **R.**
Oh, that today you would hear his voice: "Harden not your hearts as at Meribah, as in the day of Massah in the desert, where your fathers tempted me; they tested me though they had seen my works." **R.**

Second Reading: 1 Corinthians 7:32-35

Brothers and sisters: I should like you to be free of anxieties. An unmarried man is anxious about the things of the Lord, how he may please the Lord. But a married man is anxious about the things of the world, how he may please his wife, and he is divided. An unmarried woman or a virgin is anxious about the things of the Lord, so that she may be holy in both body and spirit. A married woman, on the other hand, is anxious about the things of the world, how she may please her husband. I am telling you this for your own benefit, not to impose a restraint upon you, but for the sake of propriety and adherence to the Lord without distraction.

Alleluia: Matthew 4:16

R. Alleluia, alleluia.

The people who sit in darkness have seen a great light; on those dwelling in a land overshadowed by death, light has arisen. **R.**

Gospel: Mark 1:21-28

Then they came to Capernaum, and on the Sabbath Jesus entered the synagogue and taught. The people were astonished at his teaching, for he taught them as one having authority and not as the scribes. In their synagogue was a man with an unclean spirit; he cried out, "What have you to do with us, Jesus of Nazareth? Have you come to destroy us? I know who you are—the Holy One of God!" Jesus rebuked him and said, "Quiet! Come out of him!" The unclean spirit convulsed him and with a loud cry came out of him. All were amazed and asked one another, "What is this? A new teaching with authority. He commands even the unclean spirits and they obey him." His fame spread everywhere throughout the whole region of Galilee.

FEBRUARY

FEAST OF THE PRESENTATION OF THE LORD

First Reading: Malachi 3:1-4

Thus says the Lord God: Lo, I am sending my messenger to prepare the way before me; and suddenly there will come to the temple the LORD whom you seek, and the messenger of the covenant whom you desire. Yes, he is coming, says the LORD of hosts. But who will endure the day of his coming? And who can stand when he appears? For he is like the refiner's fire, or like the fuller's lye. He will sit refining and purifying silver, and he will purify the sons of Levi, Refining them like gold or like silver that they may offer due sacrifice to the LORD. Then the sacrifice of Judah and Jerusalem will please the LORD, as in the days of old, as in years gone by.

Responsorial Psalm: Psalm 24:7, 8, 9, 10

R. (8) Who is this king of glory? It is the Lord!

Lift up, O gates, your lintels; reach up, you ancient portals, that the king of glory may come in! **R.**

Who is this king of glory? The LORD, strong and mighty, the LORD, mighty in battle. **R.**

Lift up, O gates, your lintels; reach up, you ancient portals, that the king of glory may come in! **R.**

Who is this king of glory? The LORD of hosts; he is the king of glory. **R.**

Second Reading: Hebrews 2:14-18

Since the children share in blood and flesh, Jesus likewise shared in them, that through death he might destroy the one who has the power of death, that is, the Devil, and free those who through fear of death had been subject to slavery all their life. Surely he did not help angels but rather the descendants of Abraham; therefore, he had to become like his brothers and sisters in every way, that he might be a merciful and faithful high priest before God to expiate the sins of the people. Because he himself was tested through what he suffered, he is able to help those who are being tested.

Alleluia: Luke 2:32

R. Alleluia, alleluia.

A light of revelation to the Gentiles, and glory for your people Israel. **R.**

Gospel: Luke 2:22-40 or Luke 2:22-32

Luke 2:22-40

When the days were completed for their purification according to the law of Moses, Mary and Joseph took Jesus up to Jerusalem to present him to the Lord, just as it is written in the law of the Lord, *Every male that opens the womb shall be consecrated to the Lord*, and to offer the sacrifice of *a pair of turtledoves or two young pigeons,* in accordance with the dictate in the law of the Lord. Now there was a man in Jerusalem whose name was Simeon. This man was righteous and devout, awaiting the consolation of Israel, and the Holy Spirit was upon him. It had been revealed to him by the Holy Spirit that he should not see death before he had seen the Christ of the Lord. He came in the Spirit into the temple; and when the parents brought in the child Jesus to perform the custom of the law in regard to him, he took him into his arms and blessed God, saying: "Now, Master, you may let your servant go in peace, according to your word, for my eyes have seen your salvation, which you prepared in the sight of all the peoples: a light for revelation to the Gentiles, and glory for your people Israel." The child's father and mother were amazed at what was said about him; and Simeon blessed them and said to Mary his mother, "Behold, this child is destined for the fall and rise of many in Israel, and to be a sign that will be contradicted -and you yourself a sword will pierce- so that the thoughts of many hearts may be revealed." There was also a prophetess, Anna, the daughter of Phanuel, of the tribe of Asher. She was advanced in years, having lived seven years with her husband after her marriage, and then as a widow until she was eighty-four. She never left the temple, but worshiped night and day with fasting and prayer. And coming forward at that very time, she gave thanks to God and spoke about the child to all who were awaiting the redemption of Jerusalem. When they had fulfilled all the prescriptions of the law of the Lord, they returned to Galilee, to their own town of Nazareth. The child grew and became strong, filled with wisdom; and the favor of God was upon him.

Or:

Luke 2:22-32

When the days were completed for their purification according to the law of Moses, Mary and Joseph took Jesus up to Jerusalem to present him to the Lord, just as it is written in the law of the Lord, *Every male that opens the womb shall be consecrated to the Lord,* and to offer the sacrifice of *a pair of turtledoves or two young pigeons,* in accordance with the dictate in the law of the Lord. Now there was a man in Jerusalem whose name was Simeon. This man was righteous and devout, awaiting the consolation of Israel, and the Holy

Spirit was upon him. It had been revealed to him by the Holy Spirit that he should not see death before he had seen the Christ of the Lord. He came in the Spirit into the temple; and when the parents brought in the child Jesus to perform the custom of the law in regard to him, he took him into his arms and blessed God, saying: "Now, Master, you may let your servant go in peace, according to your word, for my eyes have seen your salvation, which you prepared in the sight of all the peoples: a light for revelation to the Gentiles, and glory for your people Israel."

SUNDAY, FEBRUARY 7
FIFTH SUNDAY IN ORDINARY TIME
First Reading: Job 7:1-4, 6-7

Job spoke, saying: Is not man's life on earth a drudgery? Are not his days those of hirelings? He is a slave who longs for the shade, a hireling who waits for his wages. So I have been assigned months of misery, and troubled nights have been allotted to me. If in bed I say, "When shall I arise?" then the night drags on; I am filled with restlessness until the dawn. My days are swifter than a weaver's shuttle; they come to an end without hope. Remember that my life is like the wind; I shall not see happiness again.

Responsorial Psalm: Psalm 147:1-2, 3-4, 5-6

R. (3a) Praise the Lord, who heals the brokenhearted.

Or:

R. Alleluia.

Praise the LORD, for he is good; sing praise to our God, for he is gracious; it is fitting to praise him. The LORD rebuilds Jerusalem; the dispersed of Israel he gathers. **R.**

He heals the brokenhearted and binds up their wounds. He tells the number of the stars; he calls each by name. **R.**

Great is our Lord and mighty in power; to his wisdom there is no limit. The LORD sustains the lowly; the wicked he casts to the ground. **R.**

Second Reading: 1 Corinthians 9:16-19, 22-23

Brothers and sisters: If I preach the gospel, this is no reason for me to boast, for an obligation has been imposed on me, and woe to me if I do not preach it! If I do so willingly, I have a recompense, but if unwillingly, then I have been entrusted with a stewardship. What then is my recompense? That, when I preach, I offer the gospel free of charge so as not to make full use of my right in the gospel. Although I am free in regard to all, I have made myself a slave to all so as to win over as many as possible. To the weak I became weak, to win over the weak. I have become all things to all, to save at least some. All this I do for the sake of the gospel, so that I too may have a share in it.

Alleluia: Matthew 8:17
R. Alleluia, alleluia.

Christ took away our infirmities and bore our diseases. **R.**

Gospel: Mark 1:29-39

On leaving the synagogue Jesus entered the house of Simon and Andrew with James and John. Simon's mother-in-law lay sick with a fever. They immediately told him about her. He approached, grasped her hand, and helped her up. Then the fever left her and she waited on them. When it was evening, after sunset, they brought to him all who were ill or possessed by demons. The whole town was gathered at the door. He cured many who were sick with various diseases, and he drove out many demons, not permitting them to speak because they knew him. Rising very early before dawn, he left and went off to a deserted place, where he prayed. Simon and those who were with him pursued him and on finding him said, "Everyone is looking for you." He told them, "Let us go on to the nearby villages that I may preach there also. For this purpose have I come." So he went into their synagogues, preaching and driving out demons throughout the whole of Galilee.

SUNDAY, FEBRUARY 14
SIXTH SUNDAY IN ORDINARY TIME

First Reading: Leviticus 13:1-2, 44-46

The Lord said to Moses and Aaron, "If someone has on his skin a scab or pustule or blotch which appears to be the sore of leprosy, he shall be brought to Aaron, the priest, or to one of the priests among his descendants. If the man is leprous and unclean, the priest shall declare him unclean by reason of the sore on his head. "The one who bears the sore of leprosy shall keep his garments rent and his head bare, and shall muffle his beard; he shall cry out, 'Unclean, unclean!' As long as the sore is on him he shall declare himself unclean, since he is in fact unclean. He shall dwell apart, making his abode outside the camp."

Responsorial Psalm: Psalm 32:1-2, 5, 11

R. (7) I turn to you, Lord, in time of trouble, and you fill me with the joy of salvation.

Blessed is he whose fault is taken away, whose sin is covered. Blessed the man to whom the LORD imputes not guilt, in whose spirit there is no guile. **R.**

Then I acknowledged my sin to you, my guilt I covered not. I said, "I confess my faults to the LORD," and you took away the guilt of my sin. **R.**

Be glad in the LORD and rejoice, you just; exult, all you upright of heart. **R.**

Second Reading: 1 Corinthians 10:31-11:1

Brothers and sisters, whether you eat or drink, or whatever you do, do everything for the glory of God. Avoid giving offense, whether to the Jews or Greeks or the church of God, just as I try to please everyone in every way, not seeking my own benefit but that of the many, that they may be saved. Be imitators of me, as I am of Christ.

Alleluia: Luke 7:16

R. Alleluia, alleluia.

A great prophet has arisen in our midst, God has visited his people. **R.**

Gospel: Mark 1:40-45

A leper came to Jesus and kneeling down begged him and said, "If you wish, you can make me clean." Moved with pity, he stretched out his hand, touched him, and said to him, "I do will it. Be made clean." The leprosy left him immediately, and he was made clean. Then, warning him sternly, he dismissed him at once. He said to him, "See that you tell no one anything, but go, show yourself to the priest and offer for your cleansing what Moses prescribed; that will be proof for them." The man went away and began to publicize the whole matter. He spread the report abroad so that it was impossible for Jesus to enter a town openly. He remained outside in deserted places, and people kept coming to him from everywhere.

SUNDAY, FEBRUARY 21
FIRST SUNDAY OF LENT
First Reading: Genesis 9:8-15

God said to Noah and to his sons with him: "See, I am now establishing my covenant with you and your descendants after you and with every living creature that was with you: all the birds, and the various tame and wild animals that were with you and came out of the ark. I will establish my covenant with you, that never again shall all bodily creatures be destroyed by the waters of a flood; there shall not be another flood to devastate the earth." God added: "This is the sign that I am giving for all ages to come, of the covenant between me and you and every living creature with you: I set my bow in the clouds to serve as a sign of the covenant between me and the earth. When I bring clouds over the earth, and the bow appears in the clouds, I will recall the covenant I have made between me and you and all living beings, so that the waters shall never again become a flood to destroy all mortal beings."

Responsorial Psalm: Psalm 25:4-5, 6-7, 8-9
R. (10) Your ways, O Lord, are love and truth to those who keep your covenant.
Your ways, O LORD, make known to me; teach me your paths, Guide me in your truth and teach me, for you are God my savior. **R.**
Remember that your compassion, O LORD, and your love are from of old. In your kindness remember me, because of your goodness, O LORD. **R.**
Good and upright is the LORD, thus he shows sinners the way. He guides the humble to justice, and he teaches the humble his way. **R.**

Second Reading: 1 Peter 3:18-22
Beloved: Christ suffered for sins once, the righteous for the sake of the unrighteous, that he might lead you to God. Put to death in the flesh, he was brought to life in the Spirit. In it he also went to preach to the spirits in prison, who had once

been disobedient while God patiently waited in the days of Noah during the building of the ark, in which a few persons, eight in all, were saved through water. This prefigured baptism, which saves you now. It is not a removal of dirt from the body but an appeal to God for a clear conscience, through the resurrection of Jesus Christ, who has gone into heaven and is at the right hand of God, with angels, authorities, and powers subject to him.

Verse before the Gospel: Matthew 4:4b

One does not live on bread alone, but on every word that comes forth from the mouth of God.

Gospel: Mark 1:12-15

The Spirit drove Jesus out into the desert, and he remained in the desert for forty days, tempted by Satan. He was among wild beasts, and the angels ministered to him. After John had been arrested, Jesus came to Galilee proclaiming the gospel of God: "This is the time of fulfillment. The kingdom of God is at hand. Repent, and believe in the gospel."

MONDAY, FEBRUARY 22

FEAST OF THE CHAIR OF SAINT PETER, APOSTLE

First Reading: 1 Peter 5:1-4

Beloved: I exhort the presbyters among you, as a fellow presbyter and witness to the sufferings of Christ and one who has a share in the glory to be revealed. Tend the flock of God in your midst, overseeing not by constraint but willingly, as God would have it, not for shameful profit but eagerly. Do not lord it over those assigned to you, but be examples to the flock. And when the chief Shepherd is revealed, you will receive the unfading crown of glory.

Responsorial Psalm: Psalm 23:1-3a, 4, 5, 6

R. (1) The Lord is my shepherd; there is nothing I shall want.

The Lord is my shepherd; I shall not want. In verdant pastures he gives me repose; beside restful waters he leads me; he refreshes my soul. **R.**

Even though I walk in the dark valley I fear no evil; for you are at my side with your rod and your staff that give me courage. **R.**

You spread the table before me in the sight of my foes; you anoint my head with oil; my cup overflows. **R.**

Only goodness and kindness follow me all the days of my life; and I shall dwell in the house of the Lord for years to come. **R.**

Alleluia: Matthew 16:18
R. Alleluia, alleluia.

You are Peter, and upon this rock I will build my Church; the gates of the netherworld shall not prevail against it. **R.**

Gospel: Matthew 16:13-19

When Jesus went into the region of Caesarea Philippi he asked his disciples, "Who do people say that the Son of Man is?" They replied, "Some say John the Baptist, others Elijah, still others Jeremiah or one of the prophets." He said to them, "But who do you say that I am?" Simon Peter said in reply, "You are the Christ, the Son of the living God." Jesus said to him in reply, "Blessed are you, Simon son of Jonah. For flesh and blood has not revealed this to you, but my heavenly Father. And so I say to you, you are Peter, and upon this rock I will build my Church, and the gates of the netherworld shall not prevail against it. I will give you the keys to the Kingdom of heaven. Whatever you bind on earth shall be bound in heaven; and whatever you loose on earth shall be loosed in heaven."

SUNDAY, FEBRUARY 28

SECOND SUNDAY OF LENT

First Reading: Genesis 22:1-2, 9a, 10-13, 15-18

God put Abraham to the test. He called to him, "Abraham!"
"Here I am!" he replied. Then God said: "Take your son
Isaac, your only one, whom you love, and go to the land of
Moriah. There you shall offer him up as a holocaust on a
height that I will point out to you." When they came to the
place of which God had told him, Abraham built an altar
there and arranged the wood on it. Then he reached out and
took the knife to slaughter his son. But the LORD's
messenger called to him from heaven, "Abraham,
Abraham!" "Here I am!" he answered. "Do not lay your
hand on the boy," said the messenger. "Do not do the least
thing to him. I know now how devoted you are to God, since
you did not withhold from me your own beloved son." As
Abraham looked about, he spied a ram caught by its horns
in the thicket. So he went and took the ram and offered it up
as a holocaust in place of his son. Again the LORD's
messenger called to Abraham from heaven and said: "I
swear by myself, declares the LORD, that because you acted
as you did in not withholding from me your beloved son, I
will bless you abundantly and make your descendants as
countless as the stars of the sky and the sands of the

seashore; your descendants shall take possession of the gates of their enemies, and in your descendants all the nations of the earth shall find blessing— all this because you obeyed my command."

Responsorial Psalm: Psalm 116:10, 15, 16-17, 18-19
R. (116:9) I will walk before the Lord, in the land of the living.
I believed, even when I said, "I am greatly afflicted."
Precious in the eyes of the LORD is the death of his faithful ones. **R.**
O LORD, I am your servant; I am your servant, the son of your handmaid; you have loosed my bonds. To you will I offer sacrifice of thanksgiving, and I will call upon the name of the LORD. **R.**
My vows to the LORD I will pay in the presence of all his people, in the courts of the house of the LORD, in your midst, O Jerusalem. **R.**

Second Reading: Romans 8:31b-34
Brothers and sisters: If God is for us, who can be against us? He who did not spare his own Son but handed him over for us all, how will he not also give us everything else along with him? Who will bring a charge against God's chosen

ones? It is God who acquits us, who will condemn? Christ Jesus it is who died — or, rather, was raised — who also is at the right hand of God, who indeed intercedes for us.

Verse before the Gospel: Matthew 17:5

From the shining cloud the Father's voice is heard: This is my beloved Son, listen to him.

Gospel: Mark 9:2-10

Jesus took Peter, James, and John and led them up a high mountain apart by themselves. And he was transfigured before them, and his clothes became dazzling white, such as no fuller on earth could bleach them. Then Elijah appeared to them along with Moses, and they were conversing with Jesus. Then Peter said to Jesus in reply, "Rabbi, it is good that we are here! Let us make three tents: one for you, one for Moses, and one for Elijah." He hardly knew what to say, they were so terrified. Then a cloud came, casting a shadow over them; from the cloud came a voice, "This is my beloved Son. Listen to him." Suddenly, looking around, they no longer saw anyone but Jesus alone with them. As they were coming down from the mountain, he charged them not to relate what they had seen to anyone, except when the Son of

Man had risen from the dead. So they kept the matter to themselves, questioning what rising from the dead meant.

MARCH

THIRD SUNDAY OF LENT

First Reading: Exodus 20:1-17 or 20:1-3, 7-8, 12-17

In those days, God delivered all these commandments: "I, the LORD, am your God, who brought you out of the land of Egypt, that place of slavery. You shall not have other gods besides me. You shall not carve idols for yourselves in the shape of anything in the sky above or on the earth below or in the waters beneath the earth; you shall not bow down before them or worship them. For I, the LORD, your God, am a jealous God, inflicting punishment for their fathers' wickedness on the children of those who hate me, down to the third and fourth generation; but bestowing mercy down to the thousandth generation on the children of those who love me and keep my commandments.

"You shall not take the name of the LORD, your God, in vain. For the LORD will not leave unpunished the one who takes his name in vain.

"Remember to keep holy the Sabbath day. Six days you may labor and do all your work, but the seventh day is the Sabbath of the LORD, your God. No work may be done then either by you, or your son or daughter, or your male or female slave, or your beast, or by the alien who lives with you. In six days the Lord made the heavens and the earth, the sea and all that is in them; but on the seventh day he rested. That is why the LORD has blessed the Sabbath day and made it holy.

"Honor your father and your mother, that you may have a long life in the land which the LORD, your God, is giving you.

You shall not kill.

You shall not commit adultery.

You shall not steal.

You shall not bear false witness against your neighbor.

You shall not covet your neighbor's house.

You shall not covet your neighbor's wife, nor his male or female slave, nor his ox or ass, nor anything else that belongs to him."

Or:

Exodus 20:1-3, 7-8, 12-17

In those days, God delivered all these commandments: "I, the LORD am your God, who brought you out of the land of Egypt, that place of slavery. You shall not have other gods besides me.

"You shall not take the name of the LORD, your God, in vain. For the LORD will not leave unpunished the one who takes his name in vain.

"Remember to keep holy the Sabbath day.

Honor your father and your mother, that you may have a long life in the land which the Lord, your God, is giving you.

You shall not kill.

You shall not commit adultery.

You shall not steal.

You shall not bear false witness against your neighbor.

You shall not covet your neighbor's house.

You shall not covet your neighbor's wife, nor his male or female slave, nor his ox or ass, nor anything else that belongs to him."

Responsorial Psalm: Psalm 19:8, 9, 10, 11
R. (John 6:68c) Lord, you have the words of everlasting life.
The law of the LORD is perfect, refreshing the soul; the decree of the LORD is trustworthy, giving wisdom to the simple. **R.**
The precepts of the LORD are right, rejoicing the heart; the command of the LORD is clear, enlightening the eye. **R.**
The fear of the LORD is pure, enduring forever; the ordinances of the LORD are true, all of them just. **R.**
They are more precious than gold, than a heap of purest gold; sweeter also than syrup or honey from the comb. **R.**

Second Reading: 1 Corinthians 1:22-25

Brothers and sisters: Jews demand signs and Greeks look for wisdom, but we proclaim Christ crucified, a stumbling block to Jews and foolishness to Gentiles, but to those who are called, Jews and Greeks alike, Christ the power of God and the wisdom of God. For the foolishness of God is wiser than human wisdom, and the weakness of God is stronger than human strength.

Verse before the Gospel: John 3:16

God so loved the world that he gave his only Son, so that everyone who believes in him might have eternal life.

Gospel: John 2:13-25

Since the Passover of the Jews was near, Jesus went up to Jerusalem. He found in the temple area those who sold oxen, sheep, and doves, as well as the money changers seated there. He made a whip out of cords and drove them all out of the temple area, with the sheep and oxen, and spilled the coins of the money changers and overturned their tables, and to those who sold doves he said, "Take these out of here, and stop making my Father's house a marketplace." His disciples recalled the words of Scripture, *Zeal for your house will consume me.* At this the Jews answered and said to him,

"What sign can you show us for doing this?" Jesus answered and said to them, "Destroy this temple and in three days I will raise it up." The Jews said, "This temple has been under construction for forty-six years, and you will raise it up in three days?" But he was speaking about the temple of his body. Therefore, when he was raised from the dead, his disciples remembered that he had said this, and they came to believe the Scripture and the word Jesus had spoken. While he was in Jerusalem for the feast of Passover, many began to believe in his name when they saw the signs he was doing. But Jesus would not trust himself to them because he knew them all, and did not need anyone to testify about human nature. He himself understood it well.

SUNDAY, MARCH 14
FOURTH SUNDAY OF LENT
First Reading: 1 Samuel 16:1b, 6-7, 10-13a

The LORD said to Samuel: "Fill your horn with oil, and be on your way. I am sending you to Jesse of Bethlehem, for I have chosen my king from among his sons." As Jesse and his sons came to the sacrifice, Samuel looked at Eliab and thought, "Surely the LORD's anointed is here before him." But the LORD said to Samuel: "Do not judge from his appearance or from his lofty stature, because I have rejected him. Not as man sees does God see, because man sees the appearance but the LORD looks into the heart." In the same way Jesse presented seven sons before Samuel, but Samuel said to Jesse, "The LORD has not chosen any one of these." Then Samuel asked Jesse, "Are these all the sons you have?" Jesse replied, "There is still the youngest, who is tending the sheep." Samuel said to Jesse, "Send for him; we will not begin the sacrificial banquet until he arrives here." Jesse sent and had the young man brought to them. He was ruddy, a youth handsome to behold and making a splendid appearance. The LORD said, "There—anoint him, for this is the one!" Then Samuel, with the horn of oil in hand, anointed David in the presence of his brothers; and from that day on, the spirit of the LORD rushed upon David.

Responsorial Psalm: Psalm 23: 1-3a, 3b-4, 5, 6.
R. (1) The Lord is my shepherd; there is nothing I shall want.
The LORD is my shepherd; I shall not want. In verdant pastures he gives me repose; beside restful waters he leads me; he refreshes my soul. **R.**
He guides me in right paths for his name's sake. Even though I walk in the dark valley I fear no evil; for you are at my side with your rod and your staff that give me courage.

R.

You spread the table before me in the sight of my foes; you anoint my head with oil; my cup overflows. **R.**

Only goodness and kindness follow me all the days of my life; and I shall dwell in the house of the LORD for years to come. **R.**

Second Reading: Ephesians 5:8-14

Brothers and sisters: You were once darkness, but now you are light in the Lord. Live as children of light, for light produces every kind of goodness and righteousness and truth. Try to learn what is pleasing to the Lord. Take no part in the fruitless works of darkness; rather expose them, for it is shameful even to mention the things done by them in secret; but everything exposed by the light becomes visible, for everything that becomes visible is light. Therefore, it says: "Awake, O sleeper, and arise from the dead, and Christ will give you light."

Verse before the Gospel: John 8:12

I am the light of the world, says the Lord; whoever follows me will have the light of life.

Gospel: John 9:1-41 or 9:1, 6-9, 13-17, 34-38

John 9:1-41

As Jesus passed by he saw a man blind from birth. His disciples asked him, "Rabbi, who sinned, this man or his parents, that he was born blind?" Jesus answered, "Neither he nor his parents sinned; it is so that the works of God might be made visible through him. We have to do the works of the one who sent me while it is day. Night is coming when no one can work. While I am in the world, I am the light of the world." When he had said this, he spat on the ground and made clay with the saliva, and smeared the clay on his eyes, and said to him, "Go wash in the Pool of Siloam" — which means Sent —. So he went and washed, and came back able to see. His neighbors and those who had seen him earlier as a beggar said, "Isn't this the one who used to sit and beg?" Some said, "It is, "but others said, "No, he just looks like him." He said, "I am." So they said to him, "How were your eyes opened?" He replied, "The man called Jesus made clay and anointed my eyes and told me, 'Go to Siloam and wash.' So I went there and washed and was able to see." And they said to him, "Where is he?" He said, "I don't know." They brought the one who was once blind to the Pharisees. Now Jesus had made clay and opened his eyes on a Sabbath. So then the Pharisees also asked him how he was able to see. He said to them, "He put clay on my eyes, and I washed, and now I can see." So some of the Pharisees said, "This man is not from God, because he does not keep the Sabbath." But others said, "How can a sinful man do such signs?" And there was a division among them. So they said to the blind man again, "What do you have to say about him, since he opened your eyes?" He said, "He is a prophet." Now the Jews did not believe that he had been blind and gained his sight until they summoned the parents of the one who had gained his sight. They asked them, "Is this your son, who you say was born blind? How does he now see?" His parents answered and said, "We know that this is our son and that he was born blind. We do not know how he sees now, nor do we know who opened his eyes. Ask him, he is of age; he can speak for himself." His parents said this because they were afraid of the Jews, for the Jews had already agreed that if anyone acknowledged him as the Christ, he would be expelled from the synagogue. For this reason his parents said, "He is of age; question him." So a second time they called the man who had been blind and said to him, "Give God the praise! We know that this man is a sinner." He replied, "If he is a sinner, I do not know. One thing I do know is that I was blind and now I see." So they said to him, "What did he do to you? How did he open your eyes?" He answered them, "I told you already and you did not listen. Why do you want to hear it again? Do you want to become his disciples, too?" They ridiculed him and said, "You are that man's disciple; we are disciples of Moses! We know that God spoke to Moses, but we do not know where this one is from." The man answered and said to them, "This is what is so amazing, that you do not know where he is from, yet he opened my eyes. We know that God does not listen to sinners, but if one is devout and does his will, he listens to him. It is unheard of that anyone ever opened the eyes of a person born blind. If this man were not from God, he would not be able to do anything." They answered and said to him, "You were born totally in sin, and are you trying to teach us?" Then they threw him out. When Jesus heard that they had thrown him out, he found him and said, do you believe in the Son of Man?" He answered and said, "Who is he, sir, that I may believe in him?" Jesus said to him, "You have seen him, the one speaking with you is he." He said, "I do believe, Lord," and he worshiped him. Then Jesus said, "I came into this world for judgment, so that those who do not see might see, and those who do see might become blind." Some of the Pharisees who were with him heard this and said to him, "Surely we are not also blind, are we?" Jesus said to them, "If you were blind, you would have no sin; but now you are saying, 'We see,' so your sin remains.

Or:

John 9:1, 6-9, 13-17, 34-38

As Jesus passed by he saw a man blind from birth. He spat on the ground and made clay with the saliva, and smeared the clay on his eyes, and said to him, "Go wash in the Pool of Siloam" — which means Sent —. So he went and washed, and came back able to see. His neighbors and those who had seen him earlier as a beggar said, "Isn't this the one who used to sit and beg?" Some said, "It is, "but others said, "No, he just looks like him." He said, "I am." They brought the one who was once blind to the Pharisees. Now Jesus had made clay and opened his eyes on a Sabbath. So then the Pharisees also asked him how he was able to see. He said to them, "He put clay on my eyes, and I washed, and now I can see." So some of the Pharisees said, "This man is not from God, because he does not keep the Sabbath." But others said, "How can a sinful man do such signs?" And there was a division among them. So they said to the blind man again, "What do you have to say about him, since he opened your eyes?" He said, "He is a prophet." They answered and said to him, "You were born totally in sin, and are you trying to teach us?" Then they threw him out. When Jesus heard that they had thrown him out, he found him and said, "Do you believe in the Son of Man?" He answered and said, "Who is he, sir, that I may believe in him?" Jesus said to him, "You have seen him, and the one speaking with you is he." He said, "I do believe, Lord," and he worshiped him.

FRIDAY, MARCH 19
SOLEMNITY OF SAINT JOSEPH, HUSBAND OF THE BLESSED VIRGIN MARY

First Reading: 2 Samuel 7:4-5a, 12-14a, 16

The LORD spoke to Nathan and said: "Go, tell my servant David, 'When your time comes and you rest with your ancestors, I will raise up your heir after you, sprung from your loins, and I will make his kingdom firm. It is he who shall build a house for my name. And I will make his royal throne firm forever. I will be a father to him, and he shall be a son to me. Your house and your kingdom shall endure forever before me; your throne shall stand firm forever.'"

Responsorial Psalm: Psalm 89:2-3, 4-5, 27 and 29
R. (37) The son of David will live for ever.

The promises of the LORD I will sing forever; through all generations my mouth shall proclaim your faithfulness, for you have said, "My kindness is established forever"; in heaven you have confirmed your faithfulness. **R.**

"I have made a covenant with my chosen one, I have sworn

to David my servant: Forever will I confirm your posterity and establish your throne for all generations." **R**.

"He shall say of me, 'You are my father, my God, the Rock, my savior.' Forever I will maintain my kindness toward him, and my covenant with him stands firm." **R**.

Second Reading: Romans 4:13, 16-18, 22

Brothers and sisters: It was not through the law that the promise was made to Abraham and his descendants that he would inherit the world, but through the righteousness that comes from faith. For this reason, it depends on faith, so that it may be a gift, and the promise may be guaranteed to all his descendants, not to those who only adhere to the law but to those who follow the faith of Abraham, who is the father of all of us, as it is written, *I have made you father of many nations.* He is our father in the sight of God, in whom he believed, who gives life to the dead and calls into being what does not exist. He believed, hoping against hope, that he would become *the father of many nations,* according to what was said, *thus shall your descendants be.* That is why *it was credited to him as righteousness.*

Verse before the Gospel: Psalm 84:5

Blessed are those who dwell in your house, O Lord; they

never cease to praise you.

Gospel: Matthew 1:16, 18-21, 24a or Luke 2:41-51a
Matthew 1:16, 18-21, 24a

Jacob was the father of Joseph, the husband of Mary. Of her was born Jesus who is called the Christ. Now this is how the birth of Jesus Christ came about. When his mother Mary was betrothed to Joseph, but before they lived together, she was found with child through the Holy Spirit. Joseph her husband, since he was a righteous man, yet unwilling to expose her to shame, decided to divorce her quietly. Such was his intention when, behold, the angel of the Lord appeared to him in a dream and said, "Joseph, son of David, do not be afraid to take Mary your wife into your home. For it is through the Holy Spirit that this child has been conceived in her. She will bear a son and you are to name him Jesus, because he will save his people from their sins." When Joseph awoke, he did as the angel of the Lord had commanded him and took his wife into his home.

Or:
Luke 2:41-51a

Each year Jesus' parents went to Jerusalem for the feast of Passover, and when he was twelve years old, they went up according to festival custom. After they had completed its days, as they were returning, the boy Jesus remained behind in Jerusalem, but his parents did not know it. Thinking that he was in the caravan, they journeyed for a day and looked for him among their relatives and acquaintances, but not finding him, they returned to Jerusalem to look for him. After three days they found him in the temple, sitting in the midst of the teachers, listening to them and asking them questions, and all who heard him were astounded at his understanding and his answers. When his parents saw him, they were astonished, and his mother said to him, "Son, why have you done this to us? Your father and I have been looking for you with great anxiety." And he said to them, "Why were you looking for me? Did you not know that I must be in my Father's house?" But they did not understand what he said to them. He went down with them and came to Nazareth, and was obedient to them.

SUNDAY, MARCH 21
FIFTH SUNDAY OF LENT
First Reading: Jeremiah 31:31-34

The days are coming, says the LORD, when I will make a new covenant with the house of Israel and the house of Judah. It will not be like the covenant I made with their fathers the day I took them by the hand to lead them forth from the land of Egypt; for they broke my covenant, and I had to show myself their master, says the LORD. But this is the covenant that I will make with the house of Israel after those days, says the LORD. I will place my law within them and write it upon their hearts; I will be their God, and they shall be my people. No longer will they have need to teach their friends and relatives how to know the LORD. All, from least to greatest, shall know me, says the LORD, for I will forgive their evildoing and remember their sin no more.

Responsorial Psalm: Psalm 51:3-4, 12-13, 14-15
R. (12a) Create a clean heart in me, O God.
Have mercy on me, O God, in your goodness; in the greatness of your compassion wipe out my offense. Thoroughly wash me from my guilt and of my sin cleanse me. **R.**
A clean heart create for me, O God, and a steadfast spirit renew within me. Cast me not out from your presence, and your Holy Spirit take not from me. **R.**
Give me back the joy of your salvation, and a willing spirit sustain in me. I will teach transgressors your ways, and sinners shall return to you. **R.**

Second Reading: Hebrews 5:7-9

In the days when Christ Jesus was in the flesh, he offered prayers and supplications with loud cries and tears to the one who was able to save him from death, and he was heard because of his reverence. Son though he was, he learned obedience from what he suffered; and when he was made perfect, he became the source of eternal salvation for all who obey him.

Verse before the Gospel: John 12:26

Whoever serves me must follow me, says the Lord; and where I am, there also will my servant be.

Gospel: John 12:20-33

Some Greeks who had come to worship at the Passover Feast came to Philip, who was from Bethsaida in Galilee, and asked him, "Sir, we would like to see Jesus." Philip went and told Andrew; then Andrew and Philip went and told Jesus. Jesus answered them, "The hour has come for the Son of Man to be glorified. Amen, amen, I say to you, unless a grain of wheat falls to the ground and dies, it remains just a grain of wheat; but if it dies, it produces much fruit. Whoever loves his life loses it, and whoever hates his life in this world will preserve it for eternal life. Whoever serves me must follow me, and where I am, there also will my servant be. The Father will honor whoever serves me. "I am troubled now. Yet what should I say? 'Father, save me from this hour'? But it was for this purpose that I came to this hour. Father, glorify your name." Then a voice came from heaven, "I have glorified it and will glorify it again." The crowd there heard it and said it was thunder; but others said, "An angel has spoken to him." Jesus answered and said, "This voice did not come for my sake but for yours. Now is the time of judgment on this world; now the ruler of this world will be driven out. And when I am lifted up from the earth, I will draw everyone to myself." He said this indicating the kind of death he would die.

THURSDAY, MARCH 25
SOLEMNITY OF THE ANNUNCIATION OF THE LORD
First Reading: Isaiah 7:10-14; 8:10

The Lord spoke to Ahaz, saying: Ask for a sign from the Lord, your God; let it be deep as the nether world, or high as the sky! But Ahaz answered, "I will not ask! I will not tempt the Lord!" Then Isaiah said: Listen, O house of David! Is it not enough for you to weary people, must you also weary my God? Therefore the Lord himself will give you this sign:

the virgin shall be with child, and bear a son, and shall name him Emmanuel, which means "God is with us!"

Responsorial Psalm: Psalm 40:7-8a, 8b-9, 10, 11
R. (8a and 9a) Here I am, Lord; I come to do your will.
Sacrifice or oblation you wished not, but ears open to obedience you gave me. Holocausts or sin-offerings you sought not; then said I, "Behold I come." **R.**
"In the written scroll it is prescribed for me, to do your will, O my God, is my delight, and your law is within my heart!" **R.**
I announced your justice in the vast assembly; I did not restrain my lips, as you, O Lord, know. **R.**
Your justice I kept not hid within my heart; your faithfulness and your salvation I have spoken of; I have made no secret of your kindness and your truth in the vast assembly. **R.**

Second Reading: Hebrews 10:4-10
Brothers and sisters: It is impossible that the blood of bulls and goats take away sins. For this reason, when Christ came into the world, he said: "Sacrifice and offering you did not desire, but a body you prepared for me; in holocausts and sin offerings you took no delight. Then I said, 'As is written of me in the scroll, behold, I come to do your will, O God.'"

First he says, "Sacrifices and offerings, holocausts and sin offerings, you neither desired nor delighted in." These are offered according to the law. Then he says, "Behold, I come to do your will." He takes away the first to establish the second. By this "will," we have been consecrated through the offering of the Body of Jesus Christ once for all.

Verse before the Gospel: John 1:14ab
The Word of God became flesh and made his dwelling among us; and we saw his glory.

Gospel: Luke 1:26-38
The angel Gabriel was sent from God to a town of Galilee called Nazareth, to a virgin betrothed to a man named Joseph, of the house of David, and the virgin's name was Mary. And coming to her, he said, "Hail, full of grace! The Lord is with you." But she was greatly troubled at what was said and pondered what sort of greeting this might be. Then the angel said to her, "Do not be afraid, Mary, for you have found favor with God. Behold, you will conceive in your womb and bear a son, and you shall name him Jesus. He will be great and will be called Son of the Most High, and the Lord God will give him the throne of David his father, and he will rule over the house of Jacob forever, and of his

Kingdom there will be no end." But Mary said to the angel, "How can this be, since I have no relations with a man?" And the angel said to her in reply, "The Holy Spirit will come upon you, and the power of the Most High will overshadow you. Therefore the child to be born will be called holy, the Son of God. And behold, Elizabeth, your relative, has also conceived a son in her old age, and this is the sixth month for her who was called barren; for nothing will be impossible for God." Mary said, "Behold, I am the handmaid of the Lord. May it be done to me according to your word." Then the angel departed from her.

SUNDAY, MARCH 28
PALM SUNDAY OF THE LORD'S PASSION
AT THE PROCESSION WITH PALMS
Gospel: Mark 11:1-10 or John 12:12-16
Mark 11:1-10

When Jesus and his disciples drew near to Jerusalem, to Bethphage and Bethany at the Mount of Olives, he sent two of his disciples and said to them, "Go into the village opposite you, and immediately on entering it, you will find a colt tethered on which no one has ever sat. Untie it and bring it here. If anyone should say to you, 'Why are you doing this?' reply, 'The Master has need of it and will send it back here at once.'" So they went off and found a colt tethered at a gate outside on the street, and they untied it. Some of the bystanders said to them, "What are you doing, untying the colt?" They answered them just as Jesus had told them to, and they permitted them to do it. So they brought the colt to Jesus and put their cloaks over it. And he sat on it. Many people spread their cloaks on the road, and others spread leafy branches that they had cut from the fields. Those preceding him as well as those following kept crying out: "Hosanna! Blessed is he who comes in the name of the Lord! Blessed is the kingdom of our father David that is to come! Hosanna in the highest!"

Or:

John 12:12-16

When the great crowd that had come to the feast heard that Jesus was coming to Jerusalem, they took palm branches and went out to meet him, and cried out: "Hosanna! "Blessed is he who comes in the name of the Lord, the king of Israel." Jesus found an ass and sat upon it, as is written: Fear no more, O daughter Zion; see, your king comes, seated upon an ass's colt. His disciples did not understand this at first, but when Jesus had been glorified they remembered that these things were written about him and that they had done this for him.

First Reading: Isaiah 50:4-7

The Lord GOD has given me a well-trained tongue, that I might know how to speak to the weary a word that will rouse them. Morning after morning he opens my ear that I may hear; and I have not rebelled, have not turned back. I gave my back to those who beat me, my cheeks to those who plucked my beard; my face I did not shield from buffets and spitting. The Lord GOD is my help, therefore I am not disgraced; I have set my face like flint, knowing that I shall not be put to shame.

Responsorial Psalm: Psalm 22:8-9, 17-18, 19-20, 23-24

R. (2a) My God, my God, why have you abandoned me?
All who see me scoff at me; they mock me with parted lips, they wag their heads: "He relied on the LORD; let him deliver him, let him rescue him, if he loves him." **R.**
Indeed, many dogs surround me, a pack of evildoers closes in upon me; they have pierced my hands and my feet; I can count all my bones. **R.**

They divide my garments among them, and for my vesture they cast lots. But you, O LORD, be not far from me; O my help, hasten to aid me. **R.**

I will proclaim your name to my brethren; in the midst of the assembly I will praise you: "You who fear the LORD, praise him; all you descendants of Jacob, give glory to him; revere him, all you descendants of Israel!" **R.**

Second Reading: Philippians 2:6-11

Christ Jesus, though he was in the form of God, did not regard equality with God something to be grasped. Rather, he emptied himself, taking the form of a slave, coming in human likeness; and found human in appearance, he humbled himself, becoming obedient to the point of death, even death on a cross. Because of this, God greatly exalted him and bestowed on him the name which is above every name, that at the name of Jesus every knee should bend, of those in heaven and on earth and under the earth, and every tongue confess that Jesus Christ is Lord, to the glory of God the Father.

Verse before the Gospel: Philippians 2:8-9

Christ became obedient to the point of death, even death on

a cross. Because of this, God greatly exalted him and bestowed on him the name which is above every name.

Gospel: Mark 14:1-15:47 or 15:1-39
Mark 14:1-15:47

The Passover and the Feast of Unleavened Bread were to take place in two days' time. So the chief priests and the scribes were seeking a way to arrest him by treachery and put him to death. They said, "Not during the festival, for fear that there may be a riot among the people." When he was in Bethany reclining at table in the house of Simon the leper, a woman came with an alabaster jar of perfumed oil, costly genuine spikenard. She broke the alabaster jar and poured it on his head. There were some who were indignant. "Why has there been this waste of perfumed oil? It could have been sold for more than three hundred days' wages and the money given to the poor." They were infuriated with her. Jesus said, "Let her alone. Why do you make trouble for her? She has done a good thing for me. The poor you will always have with you, and whenever you wish you can do good to them, but you will not always have me. She has done what she could. She has anticipated anointing my body for burial. Amen, I say to you, wherever the gospel is proclaimed to the whole world, what she has done will be told in memory of her." Then Judas Iscariot, one of the Twelve, went off to the chief priests to hand him over to them. When they heard him they were pleased and promised to pay him money. Then he looked for an opportunity to hand him over. On the first day of the Feast of Unleavened Bread, when they sacrificed the Passover lamb, his disciples said to him, "Where do you want us to go and prepare for you to eat the Passover?" He sent two of his disciples and said to them, "Go into the city and a man will meet you, carrying a jar of water. Follow him. Wherever he enters, say to the master of the house, 'The Teacher says, "Where is my guest room where I may eat the Passover with my disciples?"' Then he will show you a large upper room furnished and ready. Make the preparations for us there." The disciples then went off, entered the city, and found it just as he had told them; and they prepared the Passover. When it was evening, he came with the Twelve. And as they reclined at table and were eating, Jesus said, "Amen, I say to you, one of you will betray me, one who is eating with me." They began to be distressed and to say to him, one by one, "Surely it is not I?" He said to them, "One of the Twelve, the one who dips with me into the dish. For the Son of Man indeed goes, as it is written of him, but woe to that man by whom the Son of Man is betrayed. It would be better for that man if he had never been born." While they were eating, he took bread, said the blessing, broke it, and gave it to them, and said, "Take it; this is my body." Then he took a cup, gave thanks, and gave it to them, and they all drank from it. He said to them, "This is my blood of the covenant, which will be shed for many. Amen, I say to you, I shall not drink again the fruit of the vine until the day when I drink it new in the kingdom of God." Then, after singing a hymn, they went out to the Mount of Olives. Then Jesus said to them, "All of you will have your faith shaken, for it is written: *I will strike the shepherd, and the sheep will be dispersed.* But after I have been raised up, I shall go before you to Galilee." Peter said to him, "Even though all should have their faith shaken, mine will not be." Then Jesus said to him, "Amen, I say to you, this very night before the cock crows twice you will deny me three times. But he vehemently replied, "Even though I should have to die with you, I will not deny you." And they all spoke similarly. Then they came to a place named Gethsemane, and he said to his disciples, "Sit here while I pray." He took with him Peter, James, and John, and began to be troubled and distressed. Then he said to them, "My soul is sorrowful even to death. Remain here and keep watch." He advanced a little and fell to the ground and prayed that if it were possible the hour might pass by him;

he said, "Abba, Father, all things are possible to you. Take this cup away from me, but not what I will but what you will." When he returned he found them asleep. He said to Peter, "Simon, are you asleep? Could you not keep watch for one hour? Watch and pray that you may not undergo the test. The spirit is willing but the flesh is weak." Withdrawing again, he prayed, saying the same thing. Then he returned once more and found them asleep, for they could not keep their eyes open and did not know what to answer him. He returned a third time and said to them, "Are you still sleeping and taking your rest? It is enough. The hour has come. Behold, the Son of Man is to be handed over to sinners. Get up, let us go. See, my betrayer is at hand." Then, while he was still speaking, Judas, one of the Twelve, arrived, accompanied by a crowd with swords and clubs who had come from the chief priests, the scribes, and the elders. His betrayer had arranged a signal with them, saying, "The man I shall kiss is the one; arrest him and lead him away securely." He came and immediately went over to him and said, "Rabbi." And he kissed him. At this they laid hands on him and arrested him. One of the bystanders drew his sword, struck the high priest's servant, and cut off his ear. Jesus said to them in reply, "Have you come out as against a robber, with swords and clubs, to seize me? Day after day I was with you teaching in the temple area, yet you did not arrest me; but that the Scriptures may be fulfilled." And they all left him and fled. Now a young man followed him wearing nothing but a linen cloth about his body. They seized him, but he left the cloth behind and ran off naked. They led Jesus away to the high priest, and all the chief priests and the elders and the scribes came together. Peter followed him at a distance into the high priest's courtyard and was seated with the guards, warming himself at the fire. The chief priests and the entire Sanhedrin kept trying to obtain testimony against Jesus in order to put him to death, but they found none. Many gave false witness against him, but their testimony did not agree. Some took the stand and testified falsely against him, alleging, "We heard him say, 'I will destroy this temple made with hands and within three days I will build another not made with hands.'" Even so their testimony did not agree. The high priest rose before the assembly and questioned Jesus, saying, "Have you no answer? What are these men testifying against you?" But he was silent and answered nothing. Again the high priest asked him and said to him, "Are you the Christ, the son of the Blessed One?" Then Jesus answered, "I am; and 'you will see the Son of Man seated at the right hand of the Power and coming with the clouds of heaven.'" At that the high priest tore his garments and said, "What further need have we of witnesses? You have heard the blasphemy. What do you think?" They all condemned him as deserving to die. Some began to spit on him. They blindfolded him and struck him and said to him, "Prophesy!" And the guards greeted him with blows. While Peter was below in the courtyard, one of the high priest's maids came along. Seeing Peter warming himself, she looked intently at him and said, "You too were with the Nazarene, Jesus." But he denied it saying, "I neither know nor understand what you are talking about." So he went out into the outer court. Then the cock crowed. The maid saw him and began again to say to the bystanders, "This man is one of them." Once again he denied it. A little later the bystanders said to Peter once more, "Surely you are one of them; for you too are a Galilean." He began to curse and to swear, "I do not know this man about whom you are talking." And immediately a cock crowed a second time. Then Peter remembered the word that Jesus had said to him, "Before the cock crows twice you will deny me three times." He broke down and wept. As soon as morning came, the chief priests with the elders and the scribes, that is, the whole Sanhedrin held a council. They bound Jesus, led him away, and handed him over to Pilate. Pilate questioned him, "Are you the king of the Jews?" He said to him in reply,

"You say so." The chief priests accused him of many things. Again Pilate questioned him, "Have you no answer? See how many things they accuse you of." Jesus gave him no further answer, so that Pilate was amazed. Now on the occasion of the feast he used to release to them one prisoner whom they requested. A man called Barabbas was then in prison along with the rebels who had committed murder in a rebellion. The crowd came forward and began to ask him to do for them as he was accustomed. Pilate answered, "Do you want me to release to you the king of the Jews?" For he knew that it was out of envy that the chief priests had handed him over. But the chief priests stirred up the crowd to have him release Barabbas for them instead. Pilate again said to them in reply, "Then what do you want me to do with the man you call the king of the Jews?" They shouted again, "Crucify him." Pilate said to them, "Why? What evil has he done?" They only shouted the louder, "Crucify him." So Pilate, wishing to satisfy the crowd, released Barabbas to them and, after he had Jesus scourged, handed him over to be crucified. The soldiers led him away inside the palace, that is, the praetorium, and assembled the whole cohort. They clothed him in purple and, weaving a crown of thorns, placed it on him. They began to salute him with, "Hail, King of the Jews!" and kept striking his head with a reed and spitting upon him. They knelt before him in homage. And when they had mocked him, they stripped him of the purple cloak, dressed him in his own clothes, and led him out to crucify him. They pressed into service a passer-by, Simon, a Cyrenian, who was coming in from the country, the father of Alexander and Rufus, to carry his cross. They brought him to the place of Golgotha — which is translated Place of the Skull —, they gave him wine drugged with myrrh, but he did not take it. Then they crucified him and divided his garments by casting lots for them to see what each should take. It was nine o'clock in the morning when they crucified him. The inscription of the charge against him read, "The King of the Jews." With him they crucified two revolutionaries, one on his right and one on his left. Those passing by reviled him shaking their heads and saying, "Aha! You who would destroy the temple and rebuild it in three days, save yourself by coming down from the cross." Likewise the chief priests, with the scribes, mocked him among themselves and said, "He saved others; he cannot save himself. Let the Christ, the King of Israel, come down now from the cross that we may see and believe." Those who were crucified with him also kept abusing him. At noon darkness came over the whole land until three in the afternoon. And at three o'clock Jesus cried out in a loud voice, "*Eloi, Eloi, lema sabachthani?*" which is translated, "My God, my God, why have you forsaken me?" Some of the bystanders who heard it said, "Look, he is calling Elijah." One of them ran, soaked a sponge with wine, put it on a reed and gave it to him to drink saying, "Wait, let us see if Elijah comes to take him down." Jesus gave a loud cry and breathed his last. The veil of the sanctuary was torn in two from top to bottom. When the centurion who stood facing him saw how he breathed his last he said, "Truly this man was the Son of God!" There were also women looking on from a distance. Among them were Mary Magdalene, Mary the mother of the younger James and of Joses, and Salome. These women had followed him when he was in Galilee and ministered to him. There were also many other women who had come up with him to Jerusalem. When it was already evening, since it was the day of preparation, the day before the sabbath, Joseph of Arimathea, a distinguished member of the council, who was himself awaiting the kingdom of God, came and courageously went to Pilate and asked for the body of Jesus. Pilate was amazed that he was already dead. He summoned the centurion and asked him if Jesus had already died. And when he learned of it from the centurion, he gave the body to Joseph. Having bought a linen cloth, he took him down, wrapped him in the linen cloth, and laid him in a tomb that had been hewn out of the rock. Then he rolled a stone against the entrance to the tomb. Mary Magdalene and Mary the mother of Joses watched where he was laid.

Or:

Mark 15:1-39

As soon as morning came, the chief priests with the elders and the scribes, that is, the whole Sanhedrin held a council. They bound Jesus, led him away, and handed him over to Pilate. Pilate questioned him, "Are you the king of the Jews?" He said to him in reply, "You say so." The chief priests accused him of many things. Again Pilate questioned him, "Have you no answer? See how many things they accuse you of." Jesus gave him no further answer, so that Pilate was amazed. Now on the occasion of the feast he used to release to them one prisoner whom they requested. A man called Barabbas was then in prison along with the rebels who had committed murder in a rebellion. The crowd came forward and began to ask him to do for them as he was accustomed. Pilate answered, "Do you want me to release to you the king of the Jews?" For he knew that it was out of envy that the chief priests had handed him over. But the chief priests stirred up the crowd to have him release

Barabbas for them instead. Pilate again said to them in reply, "Then what do you want me to do with the man you call the king of the Jews?" They shouted again, "Crucify him." Pilate said to them, "Why? What evil has he done?" They only shouted the louder, "Crucify him." So Pilate, wishing to satisfy the crowd, released Barabbas to them and, after he had Jesus scourged, handed him over to be crucified. The soldiers led him away inside the palace, that is, the praetorium, and assembled the whole cohort. They clothed him in purple and, weaving a crown of thorns, placed it on him. They began to salute him with, "Hail, King of the Jews!" and kept striking his head with a reed and spitting upon him. They knelt before him in homage. And when they had mocked him, they stripped him of the purple cloak, dressed him in his own clothes, and led him out to crucify him. They pressed into service a passer-by, Simon, a Cyrenian, who was coming in from the country, the father of Alexander and Rufus, to carry his cross. They brought him to the place of Golgotha — which is translated Place of the Skull — they gave him wine drugged with myrrh, but he did not take it. Then they crucified him and divided his garments by casting lots for them to see what each should take. It was nine o'clock in the morning when they crucified him. The inscription of the charge against him read, "The

King of the Jews." With him they crucified two revolutionaries, one on his right and one on his left. Those passing by reviled him, shaking their heads and saying, "Aha! You who would destroy the temple and rebuild it in three days, save yourself by coming down from the cross." Likewise the chief priests, with the scribes, mocked him among themselves and said, "He saved others; he cannot save himself. Let the Christ, the King of Israel, come down now from the cross that we may see and believe." Those who were crucified with him also kept abusing him. At noon darkness came over the whole land until three in the afternoon. And at three o'clock Jesus cried out in a loud voice, "*Eloi, Eloi, lema sabachthani?*" which is translated, "My God, my God, why have you forsaken me?" Some of the bystanders who heard it said, "Look, he is calling Elijah." One of them ran, soaked a sponge with wine, put it on a reed and gave it to him to drink saying, "Wait, let us see if Elijah comes to take him down." Jesus gave a loud cry and breathed his last. The veil of the sanctuary was torn in two from top to bottom. When the centurion who stood facing him saw how he breathed his last he said, "Truly this man was the Son of God!"

APRIL

EASTER SUNDAY: THE RESURRECTION OF THE LORD

First Reading: Acts 10:34a, 37-43

Peter proceeded to speak and said: "You know what has happened all over Judea, beginning in Galilee after the baptism that John preached, how God anointed Jesus of Nazareth with the Holy Spirit and power. He went about doing good and healing all those oppressed by the devil, for God was with him. We are witnesses of all that he did both in the country of the Jews and in Jerusalem. They put him to death by hanging him on a tree. This man God raised on the third day and granted that he be visible, not to all the people, but to us, the witnesses chosen by God in advance, who ate and drank with him after he rose from the dead. He commissioned us to preach to the people and testify that he is the one appointed by God as judge of the living and the dead. To him all the prophets bear witness, that everyone who believes in him will receive forgiveness of sins through his name."

Responsorial Psalm: Psalm 118:1-2, 16-17, 22-23

R. (24) This is the day the Lord has made; let us rejoice and

be glad.

Or:

R. Alleluia.

Give thanks to the LORD, for he is good, for his mercy endures forever. Let the house of Israel say, "His mercy endures forever." **R.**

"The right hand of the LORD has struck with power; the right hand of the LORD is exalted. I shall not die, but live, and declare the works of the LORD." **R.**

The stone which the builders rejected has become the cornerstone. By the has this been done; it is wonderful in our eyes. **R.**LORD

Second Reading: Colossians 3:1-4 or 1 Cor 5:6b-8
Colossians 3:1-4

Brothers and sisters: If then you were raised with Christ, seek what is above, where Christ is seated at the right hand of God. Think of what is above, not of what is on earth. For you have died, and your life is hidden with Christ in God. When Christ your life appears, then you too will appear with him in glory.

Or:

1 Corinthians 5:6b-8

Brothers and sisters: Do you not know that a little yeast leavens all the dough? Clear out the old yeast, so that you may become a fresh batch of dough, inasmuch as you are unleavened. For our paschal lamb, Christ, has been sacrificed. Therefore, let us celebrate the feast, not with the old yeast, the yeast of malice and wickedness, but with the unleavened bread of sincerity and truth.

Sequence: Victimae Paschali Laudes
Christians, to the Paschal Victim

Offer your thankful praises!

A Lamb the sheep redeems;

Christ, who only is sinless,

Reconciles sinners to the Father.

Death and life have contended in that combat stupendous:

The Prince of life, who died, reigns immortal.

Speak, Mary, declaring

What you saw, wayfaring.

"The tomb of Christ, who is living,

The glory of Jesus' resurrection;

bright angels attesting,

The shroud and napkin resting.

Yes, Christ my hope is arisen;

to Galilee he goes before you."

Christ indeed from death is risen, our new life obtaining.

Have mercy, victor King, ever reigning!

Amen. Alleluia.

Alleluia: 1 Corinthian 5:7b-8a

R. Alleluia, alleluia.

Christ, our paschal lamb, has been sacrificed; let us then feast with joy in the Lord. **R.**

Gospel: John 20:1-9

On the first day of the week, Mary of Magdala came to the tomb early in the morning, while it was still dark, and saw the stone removed from the tomb. So she ran and went to Simon Peter and to the other disciple whom Jesus loved, and told them, "They have taken the Lord from the tomb, and we don't know where they put him." So Peter and the other disciple went out and came to the tomb. They both ran, but the other disciple ran faster than Peter and arrived at the tomb first; he bent down and saw the burial cloths there, but did not go in. When Simon Peter arrived after him, he went into the tomb and saw the burial cloths there, and the cloth that had covered his head, not with the burial cloths but rolled up in a separate place. Then the other disciple also went in, the one who had arrived at the tomb first, and he saw and believed. For they did not yet understand the Scripture that he had to rise from the dead.

SUNDAY, APRIL 11
SECOND SUNDAY OF EASTER
First Reading: Acts 4:32-35

The community of believers was of one heart and mind, and no one claimed that any of his possessions was his own, but they had everything in common. With great power the apostles bore witness to the resurrection of the Lord Jesus, and great favor was accorded them all. There was no needy person among them, for those who owned property or houses would sell them, bring the proceeds of the sale, and put them at the feet of the apostles, and they were distributed to each according to need.

Responsorial Psalm: Psalm 118:2-4, 13-15, 22-24
R. (1) Give thanks to the LORD, for he is good, his love is everlasting.

Or:

R. Alleluia.

Let the house of Israel say, "His mercy endures forever." Let the house of Aaron say, "His mercy endures forever." Let those who fear the LORD say, "His mercy endures forever."

R.

I was hard pressed and was falling, but the LORD helped me. My strength and my courage is the LORD, and he has been my savior. The joyful shout of victory in the tents of the just: **R.**

The stone which the builders rejected has become the cornerstone. By the LORD has this been done; it is wonderful in our eyes. This is the day the LORD has made; let us be glad and rejoice in it. **R.**

Second Reading: 1 John 5:1-6

Beloved: Everyone who believes that Jesus is the Christ is begotten by God, and everyone who loves the Father loves also the one begotten by him. In this way we know that we love the children of God when we love God and obey his commandments. For the love of God is this, that we keep his commandments. And his commandments are not burdensome, for whoever is begotten by God conquers the world. And the victory that conquers the world is our faith. Who indeed is the victor over the world but the one who believes that Jesus is the Son of God? This is the one who came through water and blood, Jesus Christ, not by water alone, but by water and blood. The Spirit is the one that testifies, and the Spirit is truth.

Alleluia: John 20:29

R. Alleluia, alleluia.

You believe in me, Thomas, because you have seen me, says the Lord; blessed are they who have not seen me, but still believe! **R.**

Gospel: John 20:19-31

On the evening of that first day of the week, when the doors were locked, where the disciples were, for fear of the Jews, Jesus came and stood in their midst and said to them, "Peace be with you." When he had said this, he showed them his hands and his side. The disciples rejoiced when they saw the Lord. Jesus said to them again, "Peace be with you. As the Father has sent me, so I send you." And when he had said this, he breathed on them and said to them, "Receive the Holy Spirit. Whose sins you forgive are forgiven them, and whose sins you retain are retained." Thomas, called Didymus, one of the Twelve, was not with them when Jesus came. So the other disciples said to him, "We have seen the Lord." But he said to them, "Unless I see the mark of the nails in his hands and put my finger into the nailmarks and put my hand into his side, I will not believe." Now a week later his disciples were again inside and Thomas was with them. Jesus came, although the doors were locked, and stood in their midst and said, "Peace be with you." Then he said to Thomas, "Put your finger here and see my hands, and bring your hand and put it into my side, and do not be unbelieving, but believe." Thomas answered and said to him, "My Lord and my God!" Jesus said to him, "Have you come to believe because you have seen me? Blessed are those who have not seen and have believed." Now, Jesus did many other signs in the presence of his disciples that are not written in this book. But these are written that you may come to believe that Jesus is the Christ, the Son of God, and that through this belief you may have life in his name.

SUNDAY, APRIL 18
THIRD SUNDAY OF EASTER
First Reading: Acts 3:13-15, 17-19

Peter said to the people: "The God of Abraham, the God of Isaac, and the God of Jacob, the God of our fathers, has glorified his servant Jesus, whom you handed over and denied in Pilate's presence when he had decided to release him. You denied the Holy and Righteous One and asked that a murderer be released to you. The author of life you put to death, but God raised him from the dead; of this we are witnesses. Now I know, brothers, that you acted out of ignorance, just as your leaders did; but God has thus brought to fulfillment what he had announced beforehand through the mouth of all the prophets, that his Christ would suffer. Repent, therefore, and be converted, that your sins may be wiped away."

Responsorial Psalm: Psalm 4:2, 4, 7-8, 9
R. (7a) Lord, let your face shine on us.
Or:
R. Alleluia.
When I call, answer me, O my just God, you who relieve me when I am in distress; have pity on me, and hear my prayer! **R.**
Know that the LORD does wonders for his faithful one; the LORD will hear me when I call upon him. **R.**
O LORD, let the light of your countenance shine upon us! You put gladness into my heart. **R.**
As soon as I lie down, I fall peacefully asleep, for you alone, O LORD, bring security to my dwelling. **R.**

Second Reading: 1 John 2:1-5a
My children, I am writing this to you so that you may not commit sin. But if anyone does sin, we have an Advocate with the Father, Jesus Christ the righteous one. He is expiation for our sins, and not for our sins only but for those

of the whole world. The way we may be sure that we know him is to keep his commandments. Those who say, "I know him," but do not keep his commandments are liars, and the truth is not in them. But whoever keeps his word, the love of God is truly perfected in him

Alleluia: Luke 24:32
R. Alleluia, alleluia.

Lord Jesus, open the Scriptures to us; make our hearts burn while you speak to us. **R.**

Gospel: Luke 24:35-48

The two disciples recounted what had taken place on the way, and how Jesus was made known to them in the breaking of bread. While they were still speaking about this, he stood in their midst and said to them, "Peace be with you." But they were startled and terrified and thought that they were seeing a ghost. Then he said to them, "Why are you troubled? And why do questions arise in your hearts? Look at my hands and my feet, that it is I myself. Touch me and see, because a ghost does not have flesh and bones as you can see I have." And as he said this, he showed them his hands and his feet. While they were still incredulous for joy and were amazed, he asked them, "Have you anything here to eat?" They gave him a piece of baked fish; he took it and ate it in front of them. He said to them, "These are my words that I spoke to you while I was still with you, that everything written about me in the Law of Moses and in the prophets and psalms must be fulfilled." Then he opened their minds to understand the Scriptures. And he said to them, "Thus it is written that the Christ would suffer and rise from the dead on the third day and that repentance, for the forgiveness of sins, would be preached in his name to all the nations, beginning from Jerusalem. You are witnesses of these things."

SUNDAY, APRIL 25
FOURTH SUNDAY OF EASTER
First Reading: Acts 4:8-12

Peter, filled with the Holy Spirit, said: "Leaders of the people and elders: If we are being examined today about a good deed done to a cripple, namely, by what means he was saved, then all of you and all the people of Israel should know that it was in the name of Jesus Christ the Nazorean whom you crucified, whom God raised from the dead; in his name this man stands before you healed. He is *the stone rejected by you, the builders, which has become the cornerstone.* There is no salvation through anyone else, nor is there any other name under heaven given to the human race by which we are to be saved."

Responsorial Psalm: Psalm 118:1, 8-9, 21-23, 26, 28, 29

R. (22) The stone rejected by the builders has become the cornerstone.

Or:

R. Alleluia.

Give thanks to the LORD, for he is good, for his mercy endures forever. It is better to take refuge in the LORD than to trust in man. It is better to take refuge in the LORD than to trust in princes. **R.**

I will give thanks to you, for you have answered me and have been my savior. The stone which the builders rejected has become the cornerstone. By the LORD has this been done; it is wonderful in our eyes. **R.**

Blessed is he who comes in the name of the LORD; we bless you from the house of the LORD. I will give thanks to you, for you have answered me and have been my savior. Give thanks to the LORD, for he is good; for his kindness endures forever. **R.**

Second Reading: 1 John 3:1-2

Beloved: See what love the Father has bestowed on us that we may be called the children of God. Yet so we are. The reason the world does not know us is that it did not know him. Beloved, we are God's children now; what we shall be has not yet been revealed. We do know that when it is revealed we shall be like him, for we shall see him as he is.

Alleluia: John 10:14
R. Alleluia, alleluia.

I am the good shepherd, says the Lord; I know my sheep, and mine know me. **R.**

Gospel: John 10:11-18

Jesus said: "I am the good shepherd. A good shepherd lays down his life for the sheep. A hired man, who is not a shepherd and whose sheep are not his own, sees a wolf coming and leaves the sheep and runs away, and the wolf catches and scatters them. This is because he works for pay and has no concern for the sheep. I am the good shepherd, and I know mine and mine know me, just as the Father knows me and I know the Father; and I will lay down my life for the sheep. I have other sheep that do not belong to this fold. These also I must lead, and they will hear my voice, and there will be one flock, one shepherd. This is why the Father loves me, because I lay down my life in order to take it up again. No one takes it from me, but I lay it down on my own. I have power to lay it down, and power to take it up again. This command I have received from my Father."

MAY

FIFTH SUNDAY OF EASTER

First Reading: Acts 9:26-31

When Saul arrived in Jerusalem he tried to join the disciples, but they were all afraid of him, not believing that he was a disciple. Then Barnabas took charge of him and brought him to the apostles, and he reported to them how he had seen the Lord, and that he had spoken to him, and how in Damascus he had spoken out boldly in the name of Jesus. He moved about freely with them in Jerusalem, and spoke out boldly in the name of the Lord. He also spoke and debated with the Hellenists, but they tried to kill him. And when the brothers learned of this, they took him down to Caesarea and sent him on his way to Tarsus. The church throughout all Judea, Galilee, and Samaria was at peace. It was being built up and walked in the fear of the Lord, and with the consolation of the Holy Spirit it grew in numbers.

Responsorial Psalm: Psalm 22:26-27, 28, 30, 31-32

R. (26a) I will praise you, Lord, in the assembly of your people.

Or:

R. Alleluia.

I will fulfill my vows before those who fear the LORD. The lowly shall eat their fill; they who seek the LORD shall praise him: "May your hearts live forever!" **R.**

All the ends of the earth shall remember and turn to the LORD; all the families of the nations shall bow down before him. **R.**

To him alone shall bow down all who sleep in the earth; before him shall bend all who go down into the dust. **R.**

And to him my soul shall live; my descendants shall serve him. Let the coming generation be told of the LORD that they may proclaim to a people yet to be born the justice he has shown. **R.**

Second Reading: 1 John 3:18-24

Children, let us love not in word or speech but in deed and truth. Now this is how we shall know that we belong to the truth and reassure our hearts before him in whatever our hearts condemn, for God is greater than our hearts and knows everything. Beloved, if our hearts do not condemn us, we have confidence in God and receive from him whatever we ask, because we keep his commandments and do what pleases him. And his commandment is this: we should believe in the name of his Son, Jesus Christ, and love one another just as he commanded us. Those who keep his commandments remain in him, and he in them, and the way we know that he remains in us is from the Spirit he gave us.

Alleluia: John 15:4a, 5b
R. Alleluia, alleluia.
Remain in me as I remain in you, says the Lord. Whoever remains in me will bear much fruit. **R.**

Gospel: John 15:1-8
Jesus said to his disciples: "I am the true vine, and my Father is the vine grower. He takes away every branch in me that does not bear fruit, and every one that does he prunes so that it bears more fruit. You are already pruned because of the word that I spoke to you. Remain in me, as I remain in you. Just as a branch cannot bear fruit on its own unless it remains on the vine, so neither can you unless you remain in me. I am the vine, you are the branches. Whoever remains in me and I in him will bear much fruit, because without me you can do nothing. Anyone who does not remain in me will be thrown out like a branch and wither; people will gather them and throw them into a fire and they will be burned. If you remain in me and my words remain in you, ask for whatever you want and it will be done for you. By this is my

Father glorified, that you bear much fruit and become my disciples."

MONDAY, MAY 3
FEAST OF SAINTS PHILIP AND JAMES, APOSTLES
First Reading: 1 Corinthians 15:1-8

I am reminding you, brothers and sisters, of the Gospel I preached to you, which you indeed received and in which you also stand. Through it you are also being saved, if you hold fast to the word I preached to you, unless you believed in vain. For I handed on to you as of first importance what I also received: that Christ died for our sins in accordance with the Scriptures; that he was buried; that he was raised on the third day in accordance with the Scriptures; that he appeared to Cephas, then to the Twelve. After that, he appeared to more than five hundred brothers and sisters at once, most of whom are still living, though some have fallen asleep. After that he appeared to James, then to all the Apostles. Last of all, as to one born abnormally, he appeared to me.

Responsorial Psalm: Psalm 19:2-3, 4-5
R. (5) Their message goes out through all the earth.
Or:

R. Alleluia.

The heavens declare the glory of God; and the firmament proclaims his handiwork. Day pours out the word to day; and night to night imparts knowledge. **R.**

Not a word nor a discourse whose voice is not heard; through all the earth their voice resounds, and to the ends of the world, their message. **R.**

Alleluia: John 14:6b, 9c
R. Alleluia, alleluia.

I am the way, the truth, and the life, says the Lord; Philip, whoever has seen me has seen the Father.

Gospel: John 14:6-14

Jesus said to Thomas, "I am the way and the truth and the life. No one comes to the Father except through me. If you know me, then you will also know my Father. From now on you do know him and have seen him." Philip said to him, "Master, show us the Father, and that will be enough for us." Jesus said to him, "Have I been with you for so long a time and you still do not know me, Philip? Whoever has seen me has seen the Father. How can you say, 'Show us the Father'? Do you not believe that I am in the Father and the Father is in me? The words that I speak to you I do not speak on my own. The Father who dwells in me is doing his works. Believe me that I am in the Father and the Father is in me, or else, believe because of the works themselves. Amen, amen, I say to you, whoever believes in me will do the works that I do, and will do greater ones than these, because I am going to the Father. And whatever you ask in my name, I will do, so that the Father may be glorified in the Son. If you ask anything of me in my name, I will do it."

SUNDAY, MAY 9
SIXTH SUNDAY OF EASTER
First Reading: Acts 10:25-26, 34-35, 44-48

When Peter entered, Cornelius met him and, falling at his feet, paid him homage. Peter, however, raised him up, saying, "Get up. I myself am also a human being." Then Peter proceeded to speak and said, "In truth, I see that God shows no partiality. Rather, in every nation whoever fears him and acts uprightly is acceptable to him." While Peter was still speaking these things, the Holy Spirit fell upon all who were listening to the word. The circumcised believers who had accompanied Peter were astounded that the gift of the Holy Spirit should have been poured out on the Gentiles also, for they could hear them speaking in tongues and glorifying God. Then Peter responded, "Can anyone withhold the water for baptizing these people, who have received the Holy Spirit even as we have?" He ordered them to be baptized in the name of Jesus Christ.

Responsorial Psalm: Psalm 98:1, 2-3, 3-4
R. (2b) The Lord has revealed to the nations his saving power.
Or:
R. Alleluia.
Sing to the LORD a new song, for he has done wondrous deeds; His right hand has won victory for him, his holy arm. **R.**
The LORD has made his salvation known: in the sight of the nations he has revealed his justice. He has remembered his kindness and his faithfulness toward the house of Israel. **R.**
All the ends of the earth have seen the salvation by our God. Sing joyfully to the LORD, all you lands; break into song; sing praise. **R.**

Second Reading: 1 John 4:7-10
Beloved, let us love one another, because love is of God; everyone who loves is begotten by God and knows God. Whoever is without love does not know God, for God is love. In this way the love of God was revealed to us: God

sent his only Son into the world so that we might have life through him. In this is love: not that we have loved God, but that he loved us and sent his Son as expiation for our sins.

Alleluia: John 14:23

R. Alleluia, alleluia.

Whoever loves me will keep my word, says the Lord, and my Father will love him and we will come to him. **R.**

Gospel: John 15:9-17

Jesus said to his disciples: "As the Father loves me, so I also love you. Remain in my love. If you keep my commandments, you will remain in my love, just as I have kept my Father's commandments and remain in his love. "I have told you this so that my joy may be in you and your joy might be complete. This is my commandment: love one another as I love you. No one has greater love than this, to lay down one's life for one's friends. You are my friends if you do what I command you. I no longer call you slaves, because a slave does not know what his master is doing. I have called you friends, because I have told you everything I have heard from my Father. It was not you who chose me, but I who chose you and appointed you to go and bear fruit that will remain, so that whatever you ask the Father in my name he may give you. This I command you: love one another."

THURSDAY, MAY 13
SOLEMNITY OF THE ASCENSION OF THE LORD OR THURSDAY OF THE SIXTH WEEK OF EASTER

SOLEMNITY OF THE ASCENSION OF THE LORD
First Reading: Acts 1:1-11

In the first book, Theophilus, I dealt with all that Jesus did and taught until the day he was taken up, after giving instructions through the Holy Spirit to the apostles whom he had chosen. He presented himself alive to them by many proofs after he had suffered, appearing to them during forty days and speaking about the kingdom of God. While meeting with them, he enjoined them not to depart from Jerusalem, but to wait for "the promise of the Father about which you have heard me speak; for John baptized with water, but in a few days you will be baptized with the Holy Spirit." When they had gathered together they asked him, "Lord, are you at this time going to restore the kingdom to Israel?" He answered them, "It is not for you to know the times or seasons that the Father has established by his own authority. But you will receive power when the Holy Spirit comes upon you, and you will be my witnesses in Jerusalem, throughout Judea and Samaria, and to the ends of the earth." When he had said this, as they were looking on, he was lifted up, and a cloud took him from their sight. While they were looking intently at the sky as he was going, suddenly two men dressed in white garments stood beside them. They said, "Men of Galilee, why are you standing there looking at the sky? This Jesus who has been taken up from you into heaven will return in the same way as you have seen him going into heaven."

Responsorial Psalm: Psalm 47:2-3, 6-7, 8-9

R. (6) God mounts his throne to shouts of joy: a blare of trumpets for the Lord.

Or:

R. Alleluia.

All you peoples, clap your hands, shout to God with cries of gladness, For the LORD, the Most High, the awesome, is the great king over all the earth. **R.**

God mounts his throne amid shouts of joy; the LORD, amid trumpet blasts. Sing praise to God, sing praise; sing praise to our king, sing praise. **R.**

For king of all the earth is God; sing hymns of praise. God reigns over the nations, God sits upon his holy throne. **R.**

Second Reading: Ephesians 1:17-23 or 4:1-13 or 4:1-7, 11-13

Ephesians 1:17-23

Brothers and sisters: May the God of our Lord Jesus Christ, the Father of glory, give you a Spirit of wisdom and revelation resulting in knowledge of him. May the eyes of your hearts be enlightened, that you may know what is the hope that belongs to his call, what are the riches of glory in his inheritance among the holy ones, and what is the surpassing greatness of his power for us who believe, in accord with the exercise of his great might, which he worked in Christ, raising him from the dead and seating him at his right hand in the heavens, far above every principality, authority, power, and dominion, and every name that is named not only in this age but also in the one to come. And he put all things beneath his feet and gave him as head over all things to the church, which is his body, the fullness of the one who fills all things in every way.

Or:

Ephesians 4:1-13

Brothers and sisters, I, a prisoner for the Lord, urge you to live in a manner worthy of the call you have received, with all humility and gentleness, with patience, bearing with one another through love, striving to preserve the unity of the spirit through the bond of peace: one body and one Spirit, as you were also called to the one hope of your call; one Lord, one faith, one baptism; one God and Father of all, who is over all and through all and in all. But grace was given to each of us according to the measure of Christ's gift. Therefore, it says: *He ascended on high and took prisoners captive; he gave gifts to men.* What does "he ascended" mean except that he also descended into the lower regions of the earth? The one who descended is also the one who ascended far above all the heavens, that he might fill all things. And he gave some as apostles, others as prophets, others as evangelists, others as pastors and teachers, to equip the holy ones for the work of ministry, for building up the body of Christ, until we all attain to the unity of faith and knowledge of the Son of God, to mature to manhood, to the extent of the full stature of Christ.

Or

Ephesians 4:1-7, 11-13

Brothers and sisters, I, a prisoner for the Lord, urge you to live in a manner worthy of the calling you have received, with all humility and gentleness, with patience, bearing with one another through love, striving to preserve the unity of the Spirit through the bond of peace: one body and one

Spirit, as you were also called to the one hope of your calling; one Lord, one faith, one baptism; one God and Father of all, who is over all and through all and in all. But grace was given to each of us according to the measure of Christ's gift. And he gave some as apostles, others as prophets, others as evangelists, others as pastors and teachers, to equip the holy ones for the work of ministry, for building up the body of Christ, until we all attain to the unity of faith and knowledge of the Son of God, to mature to manhood, to the extent of the full stature of Christ.

Alleluia: Matthew 28:19ab, 20b
R. Alleluia, alleluia.
Go and teach all nations, says the Lord; I am with you always, until the end of the world. **R.**

Gospel: Mark 16:15-20
Jesus said to his disciples: "Go into the whole world and proclaim the gospel to every creature. Whoever believes and is baptized will be saved; whoever does not believe will be condemned. These signs will accompany those who believe: in my name they will drive out demons, they will speak new languages. They will pick up serpents with their hands, and if they drink any deadly thing, it will not harm them. They

will lay hands on the sick, and they will recover." So then the Lord Jesus, after he spoke to them, was taken up into heaven and took his seat at the right hand of God. But they went forth and preached everywhere, while the Lord worked with them and confirmed the word through accompanying signs.

THURSDAY OF THE SIXTH WEEK OF EASTER

(The following readings are used on this Thursday if the celebration of Ascension is transferred to the Seventh Sunday of Easter)

First Reading: Acts 18:1-8

Paul left Athens and went to Corinth. There he met a Jew named Aquila, a native of Pontus, who had recently come from Italy with his wife Priscilla because Claudius had ordered all the Jews to leave Rome. He went to visit them and, because he practiced the same trade, stayed with them and worked, for they were tentmakers by trade. Every Sabbath, he entered into discussions in the synagogue, attempting to convince both Jews and Greeks. When Silas and Timothy came down from Macedonia, Paul began to occupy himself totally with preaching the word, testifying to the Jews that the Christ was Jesus. When they opposed him and reviled him, he shook out his garments and said to them, "Your blood be on your heads! I am clear of responsibility. From now on I will go to the Gentiles." So he left there and went to a house belonging to a man named Titus Justus, a worshiper of God; his house was next to a synagogue. Crispus, the synagogue official, came to believe in the Lord along with his entire household, and many of the Corinthians who heard believed and were baptized.

Responsorial Psalm: Psalm 98:1, 2-3ab, 3cd-4
R. (2b) The Lord has revealed to the nations his saving power.
Or:
R. Alleluia.
Sing to the LORD a new song, for he has done wondrous deeds; His right hand has won victory for him, his holy arm. **R.**
The LORD has made his salvation known: in the sight of the nations he has revealed his justice. He has remembered his kindness and his faithfulness toward the house of Israel. **R.**
All the ends of the earth have seen the salvation by our God. Sing joyfully to the LORD, all you lands; break into song; sing praise. **R.**

Alleluia: John 14:18
R. Alleluia, alleluia.

I will not leave you orphans, says the Lord; I will come back to you, and your hearts will rejoice. **R.**

Gospel: John 16:16-20

Jesus said to his disciples: "A little while and you will no longer see me, and again a little while later and you will see me." So some of his disciples said to one another, "What does this mean that he is saying to us, 'A little while and you will not see me, and again a little while and you will see me,' and 'Because I am going to the Father'?" So they said, "What is this 'little while' of which he speaks? We do not know what he means." Jesus knew that they wanted to ask him, so he said to them, "Are you discussing with one another what I said, 'A little while and you will not see me, and again a little while and you will see me'? Amen, amen, I say to you, you will weep and mourn, while the world rejoices; you will grieve, but your grief will become joy."

FRIDAY, MAY 14
FEAST OF SAINT MATTHIAS, APOSTLE
First Reading: Acts 1:15-17, 20-26

Peter stood up in the midst of the brothers and sisters (there was a group of about one hundred and twenty persons in the one place). He said, "My brothers and sisters, the

Scripture had to be fulfilled which the Holy Spirit spoke beforehand through the mouth of David, concerning Judas, who was the guide for those who arrested Jesus. Judas was numbered among us and was allotted a share in this ministry. For it is written in the Book of Psalms: *Let his encampment become desolate, and may no one dwell in it.* And: *May another take his office.* Therefore, it is necessary that one of the men who accompanied us the whole time the Lord Jesus came and went among us, beginning from the baptism of John until the day on which he was taken up from us, become with us a witness to his resurrection." So they proposed two, Joseph called Barsabbas, who was also known as Justus, and Matthias. Then they prayed, "You, Lord, who know the hearts of all, show which one of these two you have chosen to take the place in this apostolic ministry from which Judas turned away to go to his own place." Then they gave lots to them, and the lot fell upon Matthias, and he was counted with the Eleven Apostles.

Responsorial Psalm: Psalm 113:1-2, 3-4, 5-6, 7-8
R. (8) The Lord will give him a seat with the leaders of his people.
Or:
R. Alleluia.

Praise, you servants of the LORD, praise the name of the LORD. Blessed be the name of the LORD both now and forever. **R.**

From the rising to the setting of the sun is the name of the LORD to be praised. High above all nations is the LORD; above the heavens is his glory. **R.**

Who is like the LORD, our God, who is enthroned on high and looks upon the heavens and the earth below? **R.**

He raises up the lowly from the dust; from the dunghill he lifts up the poor to seat them with princes, with the princes of his own people. **R.**

Alleluia: John 15:16
R. Alleluia, alleluia.

I chose you from the world, to go and bear fruit that will last, says the Lord. **R.**

Gospel: John 15:9-17

Jesus said to his disciples: "As the Father loves me, so I also love you. Remain in my love. If you keep my commandments, you will remain in my love, just as I have kept my Father's commandments and remain in his love. "I have told you this so that my joy might be in you and your joy might be complete. This is my commandment: love one another as I love you. No one has greater love than this, to lay down one's life for one's friends. You are my friends if you do what I command you. I no longer call you slaves, because a slave does not know what his master is doing. I have called you friends, because I have told you everything I have heard from my Father. It was not you who chose me, but I who chose you and appointed you to go and bear fruit that will remain, so that whatever you ask the Father in my name he may give you. This I command you: love one another."

SUNDAY, MAY 16
SOLEMNITY OF THE ASCENSION OF THE LORD OR SEVENTH SUNDAY OF EASTER

SOLEMNITY OF THE ASCENSION OF THE LORD
First Reading: Acts 1:1-11

In the first book, Theophilus, I dealt with all that Jesus did and taught until the day he was taken up, after giving instructions through the Holy Spirit to the apostles whom he had chosen. He presented himself alive to them by many proofs after he had suffered, appearing to them during forty days and speaking about the kingdom of God. While meeting with them, he enjoined them not to depart from

Jerusalem, but to wait for "the promise of the Father about which you have heard me speak; for John baptized with water, but in a few days you will be baptized with the Holy Spirit." When they had gathered together they asked him, "Lord, are you at this time going to restore the kingdom to Israel?" He answered them, "It is not for you to know the times or seasons that the Father has established by his own authority. But you will receive power when the Holy Spirit comes upon you, and you will be my witnesses in Jerusalem, throughout Judea and Samaria, and to the ends of the earth." When he had said this, as they were looking on, he was lifted up, and a cloud took him from their sight. While they were looking intently at the sky as he was going, suddenly two men dressed in white garments stood beside them. They said, "Men of Galilee, why are you standing there looking at the sky? This Jesus who has been taken up from you into heaven will return in the same way as you have seen him going into heaven."

Responsorial Psalm: Psalm 47:2-3, 6-7, 8-9
R. (6) God mounts his throne to shouts of joy: a blare of trumpets for the Lord.
Or:
R. Alleluia.

All you peoples, clap your hands, shout to God with cries of gladness, For the LORD, the Most High, the awesome, is the great king over all the earth. **R.**

God mounts his throne amid shouts of joy; the LORD, amid trumpet blasts. Sing praise to God, sing praise; sing praise to our king, sing praise. **R.**

For king of all the earth is God; sing hymns of praise. God reigns over the nations, God sits upon his holy throne. **R.**

Second Reading: Ephesians 1:17-23 or 4:1-13 or 4:1-7, 11-13
Ephesians 1:17-23

Brothers and sisters: May the God of our Lord Jesus Christ, the Father of glory, give you a Spirit of wisdom and revelation resulting in knowledge of him. May the eyes of your hearts be enlightened, that you may know what is the hope that belongs to his call, what are the riches of glory in his inheritance among the holy ones, and what is the surpassing greatness of his power for us who believe, in accord with the exercise of his great might, which he worked in Christ, raising him from the dead and seating him at his right hand in the heavens, far above every principality, authority, power, and dominion, and every name that is named not only in this age but also in the one to come. And he put all things beneath his feet and gave him as head over all things to the church, which is his body, the fullness of the one who fills all things in every way.

Or:

Ephesians 4:1-13

Brothers and sisters, I, a prisoner for the Lord, urge you to live in a manner worthy of the call you have received, with all humility and gentleness, with patience, bearing with one another through love, striving to preserve the unity of the spirit through the bond of peace: one body and one Spirit, as you were also called to the one hope of your call; one Lord, one faith, one baptism; one God and Father of all, who is over all and through all and in all. But grace was given to each of us according to the measure of Christ's gift. Therefore, it says: *He ascended on high and took prisoners captive; he gave gifts to men.* What does "he ascended" mean except that he also descended into the lower regions of the earth? The one who descended is also the one who ascended far above all the heavens, that he might fill all things. And he gave some as apostles, others as prophets, others as evangelists, others as pastors and teachers, to equip the holy ones for the work of ministry, for building up the body of Christ, until we all attain to the unity of faith and knowledge of the Son of God, to mature to manhood, to the extent of the full stature of Christ.

Or

Ephesians 4:1-7, 11-13

Brothers and sisters, I, a prisoner for the Lord, urge you to live in a manner worthy of the calling you have received, with all humility and gentleness, with patience, bearing with one another through love, striving to preserve the unity of the Spirit through the bond of peace: one body and one Spirit, as you were also called to the one hope of your calling; one Lord, one faith, one baptism; one God and Father of all, who is over all and through all and in all. But grace was given to each of us according to the measure of Christ's gift. And he gave some as apostles, others as prophets, others as evangelists, others as pastors and teachers, to equip the holy ones for the work of ministry, for building up the body of Christ, until we all attain to the unity of faith and knowledge of the Son of God, to mature to manhood, to the extent of the full stature of Christ.

Alleluia: Matthew 28:19ab, 20b
R. Alleluia, alleluia.

Go and teach all nations, says the Lord; I am with you always, until the end of the world. **R.**

Gospel: Mark 16:15-20

Jesus said to his disciples: "Go into the whole world and proclaim the gospel to every creature. Whoever believes and is baptized will be saved; whoever does not believe will be condemned. These signs will accompany those who believe: in my name they will drive out demons, they will speak new languages. They will pick up serpents with their hands, and if they drink any deadly thing, it will not harm them. They will lay hands on the sick, and they will recover." So then the Lord Jesus, after he spoke to them, was taken up into heaven and took his seat at the right hand of God. But they went forth and preached everywhere, while the Lord worked with them and confirmed the word through accompanying signs.

SEVENTH SUNDAY OF EASTER

(The following readings are used on this Seventh Sunday of Easter if Ascension of the Lord was celebrated on Thursday)

First Reading: Acts 1:15-17, 20a, 20c-26

Peter stood up in the midst of the brothers —there was a group of about one hundred and twenty persons in the one place —.He said, "My brothers, the Scripture had to be fulfilled which the Holy Spirit spoke beforehand through the mouth of David, concerning Judas, who was the guide for those who arrested Jesus. He was numbered among us and was allotted a share in this ministry. "For it is written in the Book of Psalms: *May another take his office.* "Therefore, it is necessary that one of the men who accompanied us the whole time the Lord Jesus came and went among us, beginning from the baptism of John until the day on which he was taken up from us, become with us a witness to his resurrection." So they proposed two, Judas called Barsabbas, who was also known as Justus, and Matthias. Then they prayed, "You, Lord, who know the hearts of all, show which one of these two you have chosen to take the place in this apostolic ministry from which Judas turned away to go to his own place." Then they gave lots to them, and the lot fell upon Matthias, and he was counted with the eleven apostles.

Responsorial Psalm: Psalm 103:1-2, 11-12, 19-20
R. (19a) The Lord has set his throne in heaven.
Or:
R. Alleluia.
Bless the LORD, O my soul; and all my being, bless his holy name. Bless the LORD, O my soul, and forget not all his

benefits. **R.**

For as the heavens are high above the earth, so surpassing is his kindness toward those who fear him. As far as the east is from the west, so far has he put our transgressions from us. **R.**

The LORD has established his throne in heaven, and his kingdom rules over all. Bless the LORD, all you his angels, you mighty in strength, who do his bidding. **R.**

Second Reading: 1 John 4:11-16

Beloved, if God so loved us, we also must love one another. No one has ever seen God. Yet, if we love one another, God remains in us, and his love is brought to perfection in us. This is how we know that we remain in him and he in us, that he has given us of his Spirit. Moreover, we have seen and testify that the Father sent his Son as savior of the world. Whoever acknowledges that Jesus is the Son of God, God remains in him and he in God. We have come to know and to believe in the love God has for us. God is love, and whoever remains in love remains in God and God in him.

Alleluia: John 14:18
R. Alleluia, alleluia.

I will not leave you orphans, says the Lord. I will come back to you, and your hearts will rejoice. **R**.

Gospel: John 17:11b-19

Lifting up his eyes to heaven, Jesus prayed saying: "Holy Father, keep them in your name that you have given me, so that they may be one just as we are one. When I was with them I protected them in your name that you gave me, and I guarded them, and none of them was lost except the son of destruction, in order that the Scripture might be fulfilled. But now I am coming to you. I speak this in the world so that they may share my joy completely. I gave them your word, and the world hated them, because they do not belong to the world any more than I belong to the world. I do not ask that you take them out of the world but that you keep them from the evil one. They do not belong to the world any more than I belong to the world. Consecrate them in the truth. Your word is truth. As you sent me into the world, so I sent them into the world. And I consecrate myself for them, so that they also may be consecrated in truth."

SUNDAY, MAY 23

PENTECOST SUNDAY

(At the Vigil Mass)

First Reading: Genesis 11:1-9 or Exodus 19:3-8a, 16-20b or Ezekiel 37:1-14 or Joel 3:1-5

Genesis 11:1-9

The whole world spoke the same language, using the same words. While the people were migrating in the east, they came upon a valley in the land of Shinar and settled there. They said to one another, "Come, let us mold bricks and harden them with fire." They used bricks for stone, and bitumen for mortar. Then they said, "Come, let us build ourselves a city and a tower with its top in the sky, and so make a name for ourselves; otherwise we shall be scattered all over the earth." The LORD came down to see the city and the tower that the people had built. Then the LORD said: "If now, while they are one people, all speaking the same language, they have started to do this, nothing will later stop them from doing whatever they presume to do. Let us then go down there and confuse their language, so that one will not understand what another says." Thus the LORD scattered them from there all over the earth, and they stopped building the city. That is why it was called Babel, because there the LORD confused the speech of all the world. It was from that place that he scattered them all over the earth.

Or:

Exodus 19:3-8a, 16-20b

Moses went up the mountain to God. Then the LORD called to him and said, "Thus shall you say to the house of Jacob; tell the Israelites: You have seen for yourselves how I treated the Egyptians and how I bore you up on eagle wings and brought you here to myself. Therefore, if you hearken to my voice and keep my covenant, you shall be my special possession, dearer to me than all other people, though all the earth is mine. You shall be to me a kingdom of priests, a holy nation. That is what you must tell the Israelites." So Moses went and summoned the elders of the people. When he set before them all that the LORD had ordered him to tell them, the people all answered together, "Everything the LORD has said, we will do." On the morning of the third day there were peals of thunder and lightning, and a heavy cloud over the mountain, and a very loud trumpet blast, so that all the people in the camp trembled. But Moses led the people out of the camp to meet God, and they stationed themselves at the foot of the mountain. Mount Sinai was all wrapped in smoke, for the LORD came down upon it in fire. The smoke rose from it as though from a furnace, and the whole mountain trembled violently. The trumpet blast grew louder and louder, while Moses was speaking, and God answering him with thunder. When the LORD came down to the top of Mount Sinai, he summoned Moses to the top of the mountain.

Or:

Ezekiel 37:1-14

The hand of the LORD came upon me, and he led me out in the spirit of the LORD and set me in the center of the plain, which was now filled with bones. He made me walk among the bones in every direction so that I saw how many they were on the surface of the plain. How dry they were! He asked me: Son of man, can these bones come to life? I answered, "Lord GOD, you alone know that." Then he said to me: Prophesy over these bones, and say to them: Dry bones, hear the word of the LORD! Thus says the Lord GOD to these bones: See! I will bring spirit into you, that you may come to life. I will put sinews upon you, make flesh grow over you, cover you with skin, and put spirit in you so that you may come to life and know that I am the LORD. I, Ezekiel, prophesied as I had been told, and even as I was prophesying I heard a noise; it was a rattling as the bones came together, bone joining bone. I saw the sinews and the flesh come upon them, and the skin cover them, but there was no spirit in them. Then the LORD said to me: Prophesy to the spirit, prophesy, son of man, and say to the spirit: Thus says the Lord GOD: From the four winds come, O spirit, and breathe into these slain that they may come to life. I prophesied as he told me, and the spirit came into them; they came alive and stood upright, a vast army. Then he said to me: Son of man, these bones are the whole house of Israel. They have been saying, "Our bones are dried up, our hope is lost, and we are cut off." Therefore, prophesy and say to them: Thus says the Lord GOD: O my people, I will open your graves and have you rise from them, and bring you back to the land of Israel. Then you shall know that I am the LORD, when I open your graves and have you rise from them, O my people! I will put my spirit in you that you may live, and I will settle you upon your land; thus you shall know that I am the LORD. I have promised, and I will do it, says the LORD.

Or:

Joel 3:1-5

Thus says the LORD: I will pour out my spirit upon all flesh. Your sons and daughters shall prophesy, your old men shall dream dreams, your young men shall see visions; even upon the servants and the handmaids, in those days, I will pour out my spirit. And I will work wonders in the heavens and on the earth, blood, fire, and columns of smoke; the sun will be turned to darkness, and the moon to blood, at the coming of the day of the LORD, the great and terrible day. Then everyone shall be rescued who calls on the name of the LORD; for on Mount Zion there shall be a remnant, as the LORD has said, and in Jerusalem survivors whom the LORD shall call.

Responsorial Psalm: Psalm 104:1-2, 24, 35, 27-28, 29, 30
R. (30) Lord, send out your Spirit, and renew the face of the earth.
Or:
R. Alleluia.
Bless the LORD, O my soul! O LORD, my God, you are great indeed! You are clothed with majesty and glory, robed in light as with a cloak. **R.**
How manifold are your works, O LORD! In wisdom you have wrought them all the earth is full of your creatures; bless the LORD, O my soul! Alleluia. **R.**

Creatures all look to you to give them food in due time.
When you give it to them, they gather it; when you open
your hand, they are filled with good things. **R.**

If you take away their breath, they perish and return to their
dust. When you send forth your spirit, they are created, and
you renew the face of the earth. **R.**

Second Reading: Romans 8:22-27

Brothers and sisters: We know that all creation is groaning in
labor pains even until now; and not only that, but we
ourselves, who have the first fruits of the Spirit, we also
groan within ourselves as we wait for adoption, the
redemption of our bodies. For in hope we were saved. Now
hope that sees is not hope. For who hopes for what one sees?
But if we hope for what we do not see, we wait with
endurance. In the same way, the Spirit too comes to the aid
of our weakness; for we do not know how to pray as we
ought, but the Spirit himself intercedes with inexpressible
groanings. And the one who searches hearts knows what is
the intention of the Spirit, because he intercedes for the holy
ones according to God's will.

Alleluia
R. Alleluia, alleluia.

Come, Holy Spirit, fill the hearts of the faithful and kindle in them the fire of your love. **R.**

Gospel: John 7:37-39

On the last and greatest day of the feast, Jesus stood up and exclaimed, "Let anyone who thirsts come to me and drink. As Scripture says: *Rivers of living water will flow from within him who believes in me.*" He said this in reference to the Spirit that those who came to believe in him were to receive. There was, of course, no Spirit yet, because Jesus had not yet been glorified.

PENTECOST SUNDAY
(Mass during the Day)
First Reading: Acts 2:1-11

When the time for Pentecost was fulfilled, they were all in one place together. And suddenly there came from the sky a noise like a strong driving wind, and it filled the entire house in which they were. Then there appeared to them tongues as of fire, which parted and came to rest on each one of them. And they were all filled with the Holy Spirit and began to speak in different tongues, as the Spirit enabled them to proclaim. Now there were devout Jews from every nation under heaven staying in Jerusalem. At this sound, they gathered in a large crowd, but they were confused because each one heard them speaking in his own language. They were astounded, and in amazement they asked, "Are not all these people who are speaking Galileans? Then how does each of us hear them in his native language? We are Parthians, Medes, and Elamites, inhabitants of Mesopotamia, Judea and Cappadocia, Pontus and Asia, Phrygia and Pamphylia, Egypt and the districts of Libya near Cyrene, as well as travelers from Rome, both Jews and converts to Judaism, Cretans and Arabs, yet we hear them speaking in our own tongues of the mighty acts of God."

Responsorial Psalm: Psalm 104:1, 24, 29-30, 31, 34
R. (30) Lord, send out your Spirit, and renew the face of the earth.
Or:
R. Alleluia.
Bless the LORD, O my soul! O LORD, my God, you are great indeed! How manifold are your works, O Lord! The earth is full of your creatures; **R.**
May the glory of the LORD endure forever; may the LORD be glad in his works! Pleasing to him be my theme; I will be glad in the LORD. **R.**
If you take away their breath, they perish and return to their

dust. When you send forth your spirit, they are created, and you renew the face of the earth. **R.**

Second Reading: 1 Cor 12:3b-7, 12-13 or Gal 5:16-25
1 Corinthians 12:3b-7, 12-13

Brothers and sisters: No one can say, "Jesus is Lord," except by the Holy Spirit. There are different kinds of spiritual gifts but the same Spirit; there are different forms of service but the same Lord; there are different workings but the same God who produces all of them in everyone. To each individual the manifestation of the Spirit is given for some benefit. As a body is one though it has many parts, and all the parts of the body, though many, are one body, so also Christ. For in one Spirit we were all baptized into one body, whether Jews or Greeks, slaves or free persons, and we were all given to drink of one Spirit.

Or:
Galatians 5:16-25

Brothers and sisters, live by the Spirit and you will certainly not gratify the desire of the flesh. For the flesh has desires against the Spirit, and the Spirit against the flesh; these are opposed to each other, so that you may not do what you want. But if you are guided by the Spirit, you are not under the law. Now the works of the flesh are obvious: immorality, impurity, lust, idolatry, sorcery, hatreds, rivalry, jealousy, outbursts of fury, acts of selfishness, dissensions, factions, occasions of envy, drinking bouts, orgies, and the like. I warn you, as I warned you before, that those who do such things will not inherit the kingdom of God. In contrast, the fruit of the Spirit is love, joy, peace, patience, kindness, generosity, faithfulness, gentleness, self-control. Against such there is no law. Now those who belong to Christ Jesus have crucified their flesh with its passions and desires. If we live in the Spirit, let us also follow the Spirit.

Sequence: *Veni, Sancte Spiritus*

Come, Holy Spirit, come!
And from your celestial home
Shed a ray of light divine!
Come, Father of the poor!
Come, source of all our store!
Come, within our bosoms shine.
You, of comforters the best;
You, the soul's most welcome guest;
Sweet refreshment here below;
In our labor, rest most sweet;
Grateful coolness in the heat;

Solace in the midst of woe.

O most blessed Light divine,

Shine within these hearts of yours,

And our inmost being fill!

Where you are not, we have naught,

Nothing good in deed or thought,

Nothing free from taint of ill.

Heal our wounds, our strength renew;

On our dryness pour your dew;

Wash the stains of guilt away:

Bend the stubborn heart and will;

Melt the frozen, warm the chill;

Guide the steps that go astray.

On the faithful, who adore

And confess you, evermore

In your sevenfold gift descend;

Give them virtue's sure reward;

Give them your salvation, Lord;

Give them joys that never end. Amen.

Alleluia.

Alleluia

R. Alleluia, alleluia.

Come, Holy Spirit, fill the hearts of your faithful and kindle in them the fire of your love. **R.**

Gospel: John 20:19-23 or 15:26-27; 16:12-15
John 20:19-23

On the evening of that first day of the week, when the doors were locked, where the disciples were, for fear of the Jews, Jesus came and stood in their midst and said to them, "Peace be with you." When he had said this, he showed them his hands and his side. The disciples rejoiced when they saw the Lord. Jesus said to them again, "Peace be with you. As the Father has sent me, so I send you." And when he had said this, he breathed on them and said to them, "Receive the Holy Spirit. Whose sins you forgive are forgiven them, and whose sins you retain are retained."

Or:
John 15:26-27; 16:12-15

Jesus said to his disciples: "When the Advocate comes whom I will send you from the Father, the Spirit of truth that proceeds from the Father, he will testify to me. And you also testify, because you have been with me from the beginning. "I have much more to tell you, but you cannot bear it now. But when he comes, the Spirit of truth, he will guide you to all truth. He will not speak on his own, but he will speak what he hears, and will declare to you the things that are coming. He will glorify me, because he will take from what is mine and declare it to you. Everything that the Father has is mine; for this reason I told you that he will take from what is mine and declare it to you."

SUNDAY, MAY 30
SOLEMNITY OF THE MOST HOLY TRINITY
First Reading: Deuteronomy 4:32-34, 39-40

Moses said to the people: "Ask now of the days of old, before your time, ever since God created man upon the earth; ask from one end of the sky to the other: Did anything so great ever happen before? Was it ever heard of? Did a people ever hear the voice of God speaking from the midst of fire, as you did, and live? Or did any god venture to go and take a nation for himself from the midst of another nation, by testings, by signs and wonders, by war, with strong hand and outstretched arm, and by great terrors, all of which the LORD, your God, did for you in Egypt before your very eyes? This is why you must now know, and fix in your heart, that the LORD is God in the heavens above and on earth below, and that there is no other. You must keep his statutes and commandments that I enjoin on you today, that you and your children after you may prosper, and that you may have long life on the land which the LORD, your God, is giving you forever."

Responsorial Psalm: Psalm 33:4-5, 6, 9, 18-19, 20, 22
R. (12b) Blessed the people the Lord has chosen to be his own.

Upright is the word of the LORD, and all his works are trustworthy. He loves justice and right; of the kindness of the Lord the earth is full. **R.**

By the word of the LORD the heavens were made; by the breath of his mouth all their host. For he spoke, and it was made; he commanded, and it stood forth. **R.**

See, the eyes of the LORD are upon those who fear him, upon those who hope for his kindness, to deliver them from death and preserve them in spite of famine. **R.**

Our soul waits for the LORD, who is our help and our shield. May your kindness, O LORD, be upon us who have put our hope in you. **R.**

Second Reading: Romans 8:14-17

Brothers and sisters: For those who are led by the Spirit of God are sons of God. For you did not receive a spirit of slavery to fall back into fear, but you received a Spirit of adoption, through whom we cry, "Abba, Father!" The Spirit himself bears witness with our spirit that we are children of God, and if children, then heirs, heirs of God and joint heirs with Christ, if only we suffer with him so that we may also be glorified with him.

Alleluia: Revelation 1:8
R. Alleluia, alleluia.

Glory to the Father, the Son, and the Holy Spirit; to God who is, who was, and who is to come. **R.**

Gospel: Matthew 28:16-20

The eleven disciples went to Galilee, to the mountain to which Jesus had ordered them. When they all saw him, they worshiped, but they doubted. Then Jesus approached and said to them, "All power in heaven and on earth has been given to me. Go, therefore, and make disciples of all nations, baptizing them in the name of the Father, and of the Son, and of the Holy Spirit, teaching them to observe all that I have commanded you. And behold, I am with you always, until the end of the age."

MONDAY, MAY 31

FEAST OF THE VISITATION OF THE BLESSED VIRGIN MARY

First Reading: Zeph 3:14-18a or Rom 12:9-16

Zephaniah 3:14-18a

Shout for joy, O daughter Zion! Sing joyfully, O Israel! Be glad and exult with all your heart, O daughter Jerusalem! The LORD has removed the judgment against you, he has turned away your enemies; The King of Israel, the LORD, is in your midst, you have no further misfortune to fear. On that day, it shall be said to Jerusalem: Fear not, O Zion, be not discouraged! The LORD, your God, is in your midst, a mighty savior; He will rejoice over you with gladness, and renew you in his love, He will sing joyfully because of you, as one sings at festivals.

Or:

Romans 12:9-16

Brothers and sisters: Let love be sincere; hate what is evil, hold on to what is good; love one another with mutual affection; anticipate one another in showing honor. Do not grow slack in zeal, be fervent in spirit, serve the Lord. Rejoice in hope, endure in affliction, persevere in prayer. Contribute to the needs of the holy ones, exercise hospitality.

Bless those who persecute you, bless and do not curse them. Rejoice with those who rejoice, weep with those who weep. Have the same regard for one another; do not be haughty but associate with the lowly; do not be wise in your own estimation.

Responsorial Psalm: Isaiah 12:2-3, 4bcd, 5-6
R. (6) Among you is the great and Holy One of Israel.
God indeed is my savior; I am confident and unafraid. My strength and my courage is the LORD, and he has been my savior. With joy you will draw water at the fountain of salvation. **R.**
Give thanks to the LORD, acclaim his name; among the nations make known his deeds, proclaim how exalted is his name. **R.**
Sing praise to the LORD for his glorious achievement; let this be known throughout all the earth. Shout with exultation, O city of Zion, for great in your midst is the Holy One of Israel! **R.**

Alleluia: Luke 1:45
R. Alleluia, alleluia.
Blessed are you, O Virgin Mary, who believed that what was spoken to you by the Lord would be fulfilled. **R.**

Gospel: Luke 1:39-56

Mary set out and traveled to the hill country in haste to a town of Judah, where she entered the house of Zechariah and greeted Elizabeth. When Elizabeth heard Mary's greeting, the infant leaped in her womb, and Elizabeth, filled with the Holy Spirit, cried out in a loud voice and said, "Most blessed are you among women, and blessed is the fruit of your womb. And how does this happen to me, that the mother of my Lord should come to me? For at the moment the sound of your greeting reached my ears, the infant in my womb leaped for joy. Blessed are you who believed that what was spoken to you by the Lord would be fulfilled." And Mary said: "My soul proclaims the greatness of the Lord; my spirit rejoices in God my Savior, for he has looked with favor on his lowly servant. From this day all generations will call me blessed: the Almighty has done great things for me, and holy is his Name. He has mercy on those who fear him in every generation. He has shown the strength of his arm, he has scattered the proud in their conceit. He has cast down the mighty from their thrones, and has lifted up the lowly. He has filled the hungry with good things, and the rich he has sent away empty. He has come to the help of his servant Israel for he has remembered his promise of mercy, the promise he made to our fathers, to

Abraham and his children for ever." Mary remained with her about three months and then returned to her home.

JUNE

SOLEMNITY OF THE MOST HOLY BODY AND BLOOD OF CHRIST

First Reading: Exodus 24:3-8

When Moses came to the people and related all the words and ordinances of the LORD, they all answered with one voice, "We will do everything that the LORD has told us." Moses then wrote down all the words of the LORD and, rising early the next day, he erected at the foot of the mountain an altar and twelve pillars for the twelve tribes of Israel. Then, having sent certain young men of the Israelites to offer holocausts and sacrifice young bulls as peace offerings to the LORD, Moses took half of the blood and put it in large bowls; the other half he splashed on the altar. Taking the book of the covenant, he read it aloud to the people, who answered, "All that the LORD has said, we will heed and do." Then he took the blood and sprinkled it on the people, saying, "This is the blood of the covenant that the LORD has made with you in accordance with all these words of his."

Responsorial Psalm: Psalm 116:12-13, 15-16, 17-18

R. (13) I will take the cup of salvation, and call on the name of the Lord.

Or:

R. Alleluia.

How shall I make a return to the LORD for all the good he has done for me? The cup of salvation I will take up, and I will call upon the name of the LORD. **R.**

Precious in the eyes of the LORD is the death of his faithful ones. I am your servant, the son of your handmaid; you have loosed my bonds. **R.**

To you will I offer sacrifice of thanksgiving, and I will call upon the name of the LORD. My vows to the LORD I will pay in the presence of all his people. **R.**

Second Reading: Hebrews 9:11-15

Brothers and sisters: When Christ came as high priest of the good things that have come to be, passing through the greater and more perfect tabernacle not made by hands, that is, not belonging to this creation, he entered once for all into the sanctuary, not with the blood of goats and calves but with his own blood, thus obtaining eternal redemption. For if the blood of goats and bulls and the sprinkling of a heifer's ashes can sanctify those who are defiled so that their flesh is cleansed, how much more will the blood of Christ, who through the eternal Spirit offered himself unblemished to God, cleanse our consciences from dead works to worship the living God. For this reason he is mediator of a new covenant: since a death has taken place for deliverance from transgressions under the first covenant, those who are called may receive the promised eternal inheritance.

Sequence: Lauda Sion

Laud, O Zion, your salvation,
Laud with hymns of exultation,
    Christ, your king and shepherd true:
Bring him all the praise you know,
He is more than you bestow.

    Never can you reach his due.
Special theme for glad thanksgiving
Is the quickening and the living
    Bread today before you set:
From his hands of old partaken,
As we know, by faith unshaken,

    Where the Twelve at supper met.
Full and clear ring out your chanting,
Joy nor sweetest grace be wanting,
    From your heart let praises burst:

For today the feast is holden,

When the institution olden

  Of that supper was rehearsed.

Here the new law's new oblation,

By the new king's revelation,

  Ends the form of ancient rite:

Now the new the old effaces,

Truth away the shadow chases,

  Light dispels the gloom of night.

What he did at supper seated,

Christ ordained to be repeated,

  His memorial ne'er to cease:

And his rule for guidance taking,

Bread and wine we hallow, making

  Thus our sacrifice of peace.

This the truth each Christian learns,

Bread into his flesh he turns,

  To his precious blood the wine:

Sight has failed, nor thought conceives,

But a dauntless faith believes,

  Resting on a power divine.

Here beneath these signs are hidden

Priceless things to sense forbidden;

  Signs, not things are all we see:

Blood is poured and flesh is broken,
Yet in either wondrous token
   Christ entire we know to be.
Whoso of this food partakes,
Does not rend the Lord nor breaks;
   Christ is whole to all that taste:
Thousands are, as one, receivers,
One, as thousands of believers,
   Eats of him who cannot waste.
Bad and good the feast are sharing,
Of what divers dooms preparing,
   Endless death, or endless life.
Life to these, to those damnation,
See how like participation
   Is with unlike issues rife.
When the sacrament is broken,
Doubt not, but believe 'tis spoken,
   That each severed outward token
   doth the very whole contain.
Nought the precious gift divides,
Breaking but the sign betides
   Jesus still the same abides,
   still unbroken does remain.

The shorter form of the sequence begins here.

Lo! The angel's food is given

to the pilgrim who has striven;

   see the children's bread from heaven,

   which on dogs may not be spent.

Truth the ancient types fulfilling,

Isaac bound, a victim willing,

   Paschal lamb, its lifeblood spilling,

   manna to the fathers sent.

Very bread, good shepherd, tend us,

Jesu, of your love befriend us,

   You refresh us, you defend us,

   Your eternal goodness send us

In the land of life to see.

You who all things can and know,

Who on earth such food bestow,

   Grant us with your saints, though lowest,

   Where the heavenly feast you show,

Fellow heirs and guests to be. Amen. Alleluia.

Alleluia: John 6:51

R. Alleluia, alleluia.

I am the living bread that came down from heaven, says the
Lord; whoever eats this bread will live forever. **R.**

Gospel: Mark 14:12-16, 22-26

On the first day of the Feast of Unleavened Bread, when they sacrificed the Passover lamb, Jesus' disciples said to him, "Where do you want us to go and prepare for you to eat the Passover?" He sent two of his disciples and said to them, "Go into the city and a man will meet you, carrying a jar of water. Follow him. Wherever he enters, say to the master of the house, 'The Teacher says, "Where is my guest room where I may eat the Passover with my disciples?"' Then he will show you a large upper room furnished and ready. Make the preparations for us there." The disciples then went off, entered the city, and found it just as he had told them; and they prepared the Passover. While they were eating, he took bread, said the blessing, broke it, gave it to them, and said, "Take it; this is my body." Then he took a cup, gave thanks, and gave it to them, and they all drank from it. He said to them, "This is my blood of the covenant, which will be shed for many. Amen, I say to you, I shall not drink again the fruit of the vine until the day when I drink it new in the kingdom of God." Then, after singing a hymn, they went out to the Mount of Olives.

FRIDAY, JUNE 11

SOLEMNITY OF MOST SACRED HEART OF JESUS

First Reading: Hosea 11:1, 3-4, 8c-9

Thus says the LORD: When Israel was a child I loved him, out of Egypt I called my son. Yet it was I who taught Ephraim to walk, who took them in my arms; I drew them with human cords, with bands of love; I fostered them like one who raises an infant to his cheeks; yet, though I stooped to feed my child, they did not know that I was their healer. My heart is overwhelmed, my pity is stirred. I will not give vent to my blazing anger, I will not destroy Ephraim again; For I am God and not a man, the Holy One present among you; I will not let the flames consume you.

Responsorial Psalm: Isaiah 12:2-3, 4, 5-6.

R. (3) You will draw water joyfully from the springs of salvation.

God indeed is my savior; I am confident and unafraid. My strength and my courage is the LORD, and he has been my savior. With joy you will draw water at the fountain of salvation. **R.**

Give thanks to the LORD, acclaim his name; among the nations make known his deeds, proclaim how exalted is his name. **R.**

Sing praise to the LORD for his glorious achievement; let this be known throughout all the earth. Shout with exultation, O city of Zion, for great in your midst is the Holy One of Israel! **R.**

Second Reading: Ephesians 3:8-12, 14-19

Brothers and sisters: To me, the very least of all the holy ones, this grace was given, to preach to the Gentiles the inscrutable riches of Christ, and to bring to light for all what is the plan of the mystery hidden from ages past in God who created all things, so that the manifold wisdom of God might now be made known through the church to the principalities and authorities in the heavens. This was according to the eternal purpose that he accomplished in Christ Jesus our Lord, in whom we have boldness of speech and confidence of access through faith in him. For this reason I kneel before the Father, from whom every family in heaven and on earth is named, that he may grant you in accord with the riches of his glory to be strengthened with power through his Spirit in the inner self, and that Christ may dwell in your hearts through faith; that you, rooted and grounded in love, may have strength to comprehend with all the holy ones what is the breadth and length and height and depth, and to know the love of Christ which surpasses knowledge, so that you may be filled with all the fullness of God.

Alleluia: Matthew 11:29ab or 1 John 4:10b
R. Alleluia, alleluia.

Take my yoke upon you, says the Lord; and learn from me, for I am meek and gentle of heart. **R.**

Or:

1 John 4:10b

R. Alleluia, alleluia.

God first loved us and sent his Son as expiation for our sins. **R.**

Gospel: John 19:31-37

Since it was preparation day, in order that the bodies might not remain on the cross on the Sabbath, for the Sabbath day of that week was a solemn one, the Jews asked Pilate that their legs be broken and they be taken down. So the soldiers came and broke the legs of the first and then of the other one who was crucified with Jesus. But when they came to Jesus and saw that he was already dead, they did not break his legs, but one soldier thrust his lance into his side, and immediately blood and water flowed out. An eyewitness has testified, and his testimony is true; he knows that he is speaking the truth, so that you also may come to believe. For this happened so that the Scripture passage might be fulfilled: *Not a bone of it will be broken.* And again another passage says: *They will look upon him whom they have pierced.*

SUNDAY, JUNE 13
ELEVENTH SUNDAY IN ORDINARY TIME
First Reading: Ezekiel 17:22-24

Thus says the Lord GOD: I, too, will take from the crest of the cedar, from its topmost branches tear off a tender shoot, and plant it on a high and lofty mountain; on the mountain heights of Israel I will plant it. It shall put forth branches and bear fruit, and become a majestic cedar. Birds of every kind shall dwell beneath it, every winged thing in the shade of its boughs. And all the trees of the field shall know that I, the LORD, bring low the high tree, lift high the lowly tree, wither up the green tree, and make the withered tree bloom. As I, the LORD, have spoken, so will I do.

Responsorial Psalm: Psalm 92:2-3, 13-14, 15-16
R. (2a) Lord, it is good to give thanks to you.

It is good to give thanks to the LORD, to sing praise to your name, Most High, to proclaim your kindness at dawn and your faithfulness throughout the night. **R.**

The just one shall flourish like the palm tree, like a cedar of Lebanon shall he grow. They that are planted in the house of the LORD shall flourish in the courts of our God. **R.**

They shall bear fruit even in old age; vigorous and sturdy shall they be, declaring how just is the LORD, my rock, in whom there is no wrong. **R.**

Second Reading: 2 Corinthians 5:6-10

Brothers and sisters: We are always courageous, although we know that while we are at home in the body we are away from the Lord, for we walk by faith, not by sight. Yet we are courageous, and we would rather leave the body and go home to the Lord. Therefore, we aspire to please him, whether we are at home or away. For we must all appear before the judgment seat of Christ, so that each may receive recompense, according to what he did in the body, whether good or evil.

Alleluia

R. Alleluia, alleluia.

The seed is the word of God, Christ is the sower. All who come to him will live forever. **R.**

Gospel: Mark 4:26-34

Jesus said to the crowds: "This is how it is with the kingdom of God; it is as if a man were to scatter seed on the land and would sleep and rise night and day and through it all the seed would sprout and grow, he knows not how. Of its own accord the land yields fruit, first the blade, then the ear, then the full grain in the ear. And when the grain is ripe, he wields the sickle at once, for the harvest has come." He said, "To what shall we compare the kingdom of God, or what parable can we use for it? It is like a mustard seed that, when it is sown in the ground, is the smallest of all the seeds on the earth. But once it is sown, it springs up and becomes the largest of plants and puts forth large branches, so that the birds of the sky can dwell in its shade." With many such parables he spoke the word to them as they were able to understand it. Without parables he did not speak to them, but to his own disciples he explained everything in private.

SUNDAY, JUNE 20
TWELFTH SUNDAY IN ORDINARY TIME
First Reading: Job 38:1, 8-11

The Lord addressed Job out of the storm and said: Who shut within doors the sea, when it burst forth from the womb; when I made the clouds its garment and thick darkness its swaddling bands? When I set limits for it and fastened the bar of its door, and said: Thus far shall you come but no farther, and here shall your proud waves be stilled!

Responsorial Psalm: Psalm 107:23-24, 25-26, 28-29, 30-31
R. (1b) Give thanks to the Lord, his love is everlasting.
Or:
R. Alleluia.
They who sailed the sea in ships, trading on the deep waters, these saw the works of the LORD and his wonders in the abyss. **R.**
His command raised up a storm wind which tossed its waves on high. They mounted up to heaven; they sank to the depths; their hearts melted away in their plight. **R.**
They cried to the LORD in their distress; from their straits he rescued them, He hushed the storm to a gentle breeze, and the billows of the sea were stilled. **R.**
They rejoiced that they were calmed, and he brought them to their desired haven. Let them give thanks to the LORD for his kindness and his wondrous deeds to the children of men. **R.**

Second Reading: 2 Corinthians 5:14-17
Brothers and sisters: The love of Christ impels us, once we have come to the conviction that one died for all; therefore,

all have died. He indeed died for all, so that those who live might no longer live for themselves but for him who for their sake died and was raised. Consequently, from now on we regard no one according to the flesh; even if we once knew Christ according to the flesh, yet now we know him so no longer. So whoever is in Christ is a new creation: the old things have passed away; behold, new things have come.

Alleluia: Luke 7:16
R. Alleluia, alleluia.

A great prophet has risen in our midst God has visited his people. **R.**

Gospel: Mark 4:35-41

On that day, as evening drew on, Jesus said to his disciples: "Let us cross to the other side." Leaving the crowd, they took Jesus with them in the boat just as he was. And other boats were with him. A violent squall came up and waves were breaking over the boat, so that it was already filling up. Jesus was in the stern, asleep on a cushion. They woke him and said to him, "Teacher, do you not care that we are perishing?" He woke up, rebuked the wind, and said to the sea, "Quiet! Be still!" The wind ceased and there was great calm. Then he asked them, "Why are you terrified? Do you not yet have faith?" They were filled with great awe and said to one another, "Who then is this whom even wind and sea obey?"

THURSDAY, JUNE 24
SOLEMNITY OF THE NATIVITY OF SAINT JOHN THE BAPTIST
(Vigil Mass)
First Reading: Jeremiah 1:4-10

In the days of King Josiah, the word of the LORD came to me, saying: Before I formed you in the womb I knew you, before you were born I dedicated you, a prophet to the nations I appointed you. "Ah, Lord GOD!" I said, "I know not how to speak; I am too young." But the LORD answered me, say not, "I am too young." To whomever I send you, you shall go; whatever I command you, you shall speak. Have no fear before them, because I am with you to deliver you, says the LORD. Then the LORD extended his hand and touched my mouth, saying, See, I place my words in your mouth! This day I set you over nations and over kingdoms, to root up and to tear down, to destroy and to demolish, to build and to plant.

Responsorial Psalm: Psalm 71:1-2, 3-4a, 5-6ab, 15ab and 17

R. (6) Since my mother's womb, you have been my strength.

In you, O LORD, I take refuge; let me never be put to shame. In your justice rescue me, and deliver me; incline your ear to me, and save me. **R.**

Be my rock of refuge, a stronghold to give me safety, for you are my rock and my fortress. O my God, rescue me from the hand of the wicked. **R.**

For you are my hope, O LORD; my trust, O LORD, from my youth. On you I depend from birth; from my mother's womb you are my strength. **R.**

My mouth shall declare your justice, day by day your salvation. O God, you have taught me from my youth, and till the present I proclaim your wondrous deeds. **R.**

Second Reading: 1 Peter 1:8-12

Beloved: Although you have not seen Jesus Christ you love him; even though you do not see him now yet believe in him, you rejoice with an indescribable and glorious joy, as you attain the goal of your faith, the salvation of your souls. Concerning this salvation, prophets who prophesied about the grace that was to be yours searched and investigated it, investigating the time and circumstances that the Spirit of Christ within them indicated when he testified in advance to the sufferings destined for Christ and the glories to follow them. It was revealed to them that they were serving not themselves but you with regard to the things that have now been announced to you by those who preached the Good News to you through the Holy Spirit sent from heaven, things into which angels longed to look.

Alleluia: John 1:7; Luke 1:17

R. Alleluia, alleluia.

He came to testify to the light, to prepare a people fit for the Lord. **R.**

Gospel: Luke 1:5-17

In the days of Herod, King of Judea, there was a priest named Zechariah of the priestly division of Abijah; his wife was from the daughters of Aaron, and her name was Elizabeth. Both were righteous in the eyes of God, observing all the commandments and ordinances of the Lord blamelessly. But they had no child, because Elizabeth was barren and both were advanced in years. Once when he was serving as priest in his division's turn before God, according to the practice of the priestly service, he was chosen by lot to enter the sanctuary of the Lord to burn incense. Then, when the whole assembly of the people was praying outside at the hour of the incense offering, the angel of the Lord appeared to him, standing at the right of the altar of incense. Zechariah was troubled by what he saw, and fear came upon him. But the angel said to him, "Do not be afraid, Zechariah, because your prayer has been heard. Your wife Elizabeth will bear you a son, and you shall name him John. And you will have joy and gladness, and many will rejoice at his birth, for he will be great in the sight of the Lord. John will drink neither wine nor strong drink. He will be filled with the Holy Spirit even from his mother's womb, and he will turn many of the children of Israel to the Lord their God. He will go before him in the spirit and power of Elijah to turn their hearts toward their children and the disobedient to the understanding of the righteous, to prepare a people fit for the Lord."

SOLEMNITY OF THE NATIVITY OF SAINT JOHN THE BAPTIST

(Mass during the Day)

First Reading: Isaiah 49:1-6

Hear me, O coastlands, listen, O distant peoples. The LORD called me from birth, from my mother's womb he gave me my name. He made of me a sharp-edged sword and concealed me in the shadow of his arm. He made me a polished arrow, in his quiver he hid me. You are my servant, he said to me, Israel, through whom I show my glory. Though I thought I had toiled in vain, and for nothing, uselessly, spent my strength, yet my reward is with the LORD, my recompense is with my God. For now the LORD has spoken who formed me as his servant from the womb, that Jacob may be brought back to him and Israel gathered to him; and I am made glorious in the sight of the LORD, and my God is now my strength! It is too little, he says, for you to be my servant, to raise up the tribes of Jacob, and restore the survivors of Israel; I will make you a light to the nations, that my salvation may reach to the ends of the earth.

Responsorial Psalm: Psalm 139:1b-3, 13-14ab, 14c-15
R. (14) I praise you, for I am wonderfully made.
O LORD, you have probed me, you know me: you know when I sit and when I stand; you understand my thoughts from afar. My journeys and my rest you scrutinize, with all my ways you are familiar. **R.**
Truly you have formed my inmost being; you knit me in my mother's womb. I give you thanks that I am fearfully, wonderfully made; wonderful are your works. **R.**
My soul also you knew full well; nor was my frame unknown to you When I was made in secret, when I was

fashioned in the depths of the earth. **R.**

Second Reading: Acts 13:22-26

In those days, Paul said: "God raised up David as king; of him God testified, *I have found David, son of Jesse, a man after my own heart; he will carry out my every wish.* From this man's descendants God, according to his promise, has brought to Israel a savior, Jesus. John heralded his coming by proclaiming a baptism of repentance to all the people of Israel; and as John was completing his course, he would say, 'What do you suppose that I am? I am not he. Behold, one is coming after me; I am not worthy to unfasten the sandals of his feet.' "My brothers, sons of the family of Abraham, and those others among you who are God-fearing, to us this word of salvation has been sent."

Alleluia: Luke 1:76
R. Alleluia, alleluia.

You, child, will be called prophet of the Most High, for you will go before the Lord to prepare his way. **R.**

Gospel: Luke 1:57-66, 80

When the time arrived for Elizabeth to have her child she gave birth to a son. Her neighbors and relatives heard that the Lord had shown his great mercy toward her, and they rejoiced with her. When they came on the eighth day to circumcise the child, they were going to call him Zechariah after his father, but his mother said in reply, "No. He will be called John." But they answered her, "There is no one among your relatives who has this name." So they made signs, asking his father what he wished him to be called. He asked for a tablet and wrote, "John is his name," and all were amazed. Immediately his mouth was opened, his tongue freed, and he spoke blessing God. Then fear came upon all their neighbors, and all these matters were discussed throughout the hill country of Judea. All who heard these things took them to heart, saying, "What, then, will this child be?" For surely the hand of the Lord was with him. The child grew and became strong in spirit, and he was in the desert until the day of his manifestation to Israel.

SUNDAY, JUNE 27

THIRTEENTH SUNDAY IN ORDINARY TIME

First Reading: Wisdom 1:13-15; 2:23-24

God did not make death, nor does he rejoice in the destruction of the living. For he fashioned all things that they might have being; and the creatures of the world are wholesome, and there is not a destructive drug among them nor any domain of the netherworld on earth, for justice is undying. For God formed man to be imperishable; the image of his own nature he made him. But by the envy of the devil, death entered the world, and they who belong to his company experience it.

Responsorial Psalm: Psalm 30:2, 4, 5-6, 11, 12, 13
R. (2a) I will praise you, Lord, for you have rescued me.
I will extol you, O LORD, for you drew me clear and did not let my enemies rejoice over me. O LORD, you brought me up from the netherworld; you preserved me from among those going down into the pit. **R.**
Sing praise to the LORD, you his faithful ones, and give thanks to his holy name. For his anger lasts but a moment; a lifetime, his good will. At nightfall, weeping enters in, but with the dawn, rejoicing. **R.**
Hear, O LORD, and have pity on me; O LORD, be my helper. You changed my mourning into dancing; O LORD, my God, forever will I give you thanks. **R.**

Second Reading: 2 Corinthians 8:7, 9, 13-15
Brothers and sisters: As you excel in every respect, in faith, discourse, knowledge, all earnestness, and in the love we have for you, may you excel in this gracious act also. For you

know the gracious act of our Lord Jesus Christ, that though he was rich, for your sake he became poor, so that by his poverty you might become rich. Not that others should have relief while you are burdened, but that as a matter of equality your abundance at the present time should supply their needs, so that their abundance may also supply your needs, that there may be equality. As it is written: *Whoever had much did not have more, and whoever had little did not have less.*

Alleluia: 2 Timothy 1:10
R. Alleluia, alleluia.
Our Savior Jesus Christ destroyed death and brought life to light through the Gospel. **R.**

Gospel: Mark 5:21-43 or 5:21-24, 35b-43
When Jesus had crossed again in the boat to the other side, a large crowd gathered around him, and he stayed close to the sea. One of the synagogue officials, named Jairus, came forward. Seeing him he fell at his feet and pleaded earnestly with him, saying, "My daughter is at the point of death. Please, come lay your hands on her that she may get well and live." He went off with him, and a large crowd followed him and pressed upon him. There was a woman afflicted

with hemorrhages for twelve years. She had suffered greatly at the hands of many doctors and had spent all that she had. Yet she was not helped but only grew worse. She had heard about Jesus and came up behind him in the crowd and touched his cloak. She said, "If I but touch his clothes, I shall be cured." Immediately her flow of blood dried up. She felt in her body that she was healed of her affliction. Jesus, aware at once that power had gone out from him, turned around in the crowd and asked, "Who has touched my clothes?" But his disciples said to Jesus, "You see how the crowd is pressing upon you, and yet you ask, 'Who touched me?'" And he looked around to see who had done it. The woman, realizing what had happened to her, approached in fear and trembling. She fell down before Jesus and told him the whole truth. He said to her, "Daughter, your faith has saved you. Go in peace and be cured of your affliction." While he was still speaking, people from the synagogue official's house arrived and said, "Your daughter has died; why trouble the teacher any longer?" Disregarding the message that was reported, Jesus said to the synagogue official, "Do not be afraid; just have faith." He did not allow anyone to accompany him inside except Peter, James, and John, the brother of James. When they arrived at the house of the synagogue official, he caught sight of a commotion, people weeping and wailing loudly. So he went in and said to them, "Why this commotion and weeping? The child is not dead but asleep." And they ridiculed him. Then he put them all out. He took along the child's father and mother and those who were with him and entered the room where the child was. He took the child by the hand and said to her, "*Talitha koum*," which means, "Little girl, I say to you, arise!" The girl, a child of twelve, arose immediately and walked around. At that they were utterly astounded. He gave strict orders that no one should know this and said that she should be given something to eat.

Or:

Mark 5:21-24, 35b-43

When Jesus had crossed again in the boat to the other side, a large crowd gathered around him, and he stayed close to the sea. One of the synagogue officials, named Jairus, came forward. Seeing him he fell at his feet and pleaded earnestly with him, saying, "My daughter is at the point of death. Please, come lay your hands on her that she may get well and live." He went off with him, and a large crowd followed him and pressed upon him. While he was still speaking, people from the synagogue official's house arrived and said, "Your daughter has died; why trouble the teacher any longer?" Disregarding the message that was reported, Jesus said to the synagogue official, "Do not be afraid; just have faith." He did not allow anyone to accompany him inside except Peter, James, and John, the brother of James. When they arrived at the house of the synagogue official, he caught sight of a commotion, people weeping and wailing loudly. So he went in and said to them, "Why this commotion and weeping? The child is not dead but asleep." And they ridiculed him. Then he put them all out. He took along the child's father and mother and those who were with him and entered the room where the child was. He took the child by the hand and said to her, *"Talitha koum,"* which means, "Little girl, I say to you, arise!" The girl, a child of twelve, arose immediately and walked around. At that they were utterly astounded. He gave strict orders that no one should know this and said that she should be given something to eat.

TUESDAY, JUNE 29

SOLEMNITY OF SAINTS PETER AND PAUL, APOSTLES

(Vigil)

First Reading: Acts 3:1-10

Peter and John were going up to the temple area for the three o'clock hour of prayer. And a man crippled from birth was carried and placed at the gate of the temple called "the Beautiful Gate" every day to beg for alms from the people who entered the temple. When he saw Peter and John about to go into the temple, he asked for alms. But Peter looked intently at him, as did John, and said, "Look at us." He paid attention to them, expecting to receive something from them. Peter said, "I have neither silver nor gold, but what I do have I give you: in the name of Jesus Christ the Nazorean, rise and walk." Then Peter took him by the right hand and raised him up, and immediately his feet and ankles grew strong. He leaped up, stood, and walked around, and went into the temple with them, walking and jumping and praising God. When all the people saw the man walking and praising God, they recognized him as the one who used to sit begging at the Beautiful Gate of the temple, and they were filled with amazement and astonishment at what had happened to him.

Responsorial Psalm: Psalm 19:2-3, 4-5

R. (5) Their message goes out through all the earth.

The heavens declare the glory of God; and the firmament
proclaims his handiwork. Day pours out the word to day;
and night to night imparts knowledge. **R.**

Not a word nor a discourse whose voice is not heard;
through all the earth their voice resounds, and to the ends of
the world, their message. **R.**

Second Reading: Galatians 1:11-20

I want you to know, brothers and sisters, that the Gospel
preached by me is not of human origin. For I did not receive
it from a human being, nor was I taught it, but it came
through a revelation of Jesus Christ. For you heard of my
former way of life in Judaism, how I persecuted the Church
of God beyond measure and tried to destroy it, and
progressed in Judaism beyond many of my contemporaries
among my race, since I was even more a zealot for my
ancestral traditions. But when God, who from my mother's
womb had set me apart and called me through his grace,
was pleased to reveal his Son to me, so that I might proclaim
him to the Gentiles, I did not immediately consult flesh and
blood, nor did I go up to Jerusalem to those who were
Apostles before me; rather, I went into Arabia and then

returned to Damascus. Then after three years I went up to Jerusalem to confer with Cephas and remained with him for fifteen days. But I did not see any other of the Apostles, only James the brother of the Lord. As to what I am writing to you, behold, before God, I am not lying.

Alleluia: John 21:17

R. Alleluia, alleluia.

Lord, you know everything: you know that I love you. **R.**

Gospel: John 21:15-19

Jesus had revealed himself to his disciples and, when they had finished breakfast, said to Simon Peter, "Simon, son of John, do you love me more than these?" Simon Peter answered him, "Yes, Lord, you know that I love you." Jesus said to him, "Feed my lambs." He then said to Simon Peter a second time, "Simon, son of John, do you love me?" Simon Peter answered him, "Yes, Lord, you know that I love you." He said to him, "Tend my sheep." He said to him the third time, "Simon, son of John, do you love me?" Peter was distressed that he had said to him a third time, "Do you love me?" and he said to him, "Lord, you know everything; you know that I love you." Jesus said to him, "Feed my sheep. Amen, amen, I say to you, when you were younger, you used to dress yourself and go where you wanted; but when you grow old, you will stretch out your hands, and someone else will dress you and lead you where you do not want to go." He said this signifying by what kind of death he would glorify God. And when he had said this, he said to him, "Follow me."

SOLEMNITY OF SAINTS PETER AND PAUL, APOSTLES

(Mass during the Day)

First Reading: Acts 12:1-11

In those days, King Herod laid hands upon some members of the Church to harm them. He had James, the brother of John, killed by the sword, and when he saw that this was pleasing to the Jews he proceeded to arrest Peter also. –It was the feast of Unleavened Bread. –He had him taken into custody and put in prison under the guard of four squads of four soldiers each. He intended to bring him before the people after Passover. Peter thus was being kept in prison, but prayer by the Church was fervently being made to God on his behalf. On the very night before Herod was to bring him to trial, Peter, secured by double chains, was sleeping between two soldiers, while outside the door guards kept watch on the prison. Suddenly the angel of the Lord stood by him and a light shone in the cell. He tapped Peter on the side and awakened him, saying, "Get up quickly." The chains fell from his wrists. The angel said to him, "Put on your belt and your sandals." He did so. Then he said to him, "Put on your cloak and follow me." So he followed him out, not realizing that what was happening through the angel was real; he thought he was seeing a vision. They passed the first guard, then the second, and came to the iron gate leading out to the city, which opened for them by itself. They emerged and made their way down an alley, and suddenly the angel left him. Then Peter recovered his senses and said, "Now I know for certain that the Lord sent his angel and rescued me from the hand of Herod and from all that the Jewish people had been expecting."

Responsorial Psalm: Psalm 34:2-3, 4-5, 6-7, 8-9
R. (5) The angel of the Lord will rescue those who fear him.
I will bless the LORD at all times; his praise shall be ever in my mouth. Let my soul glory in the LORD; lowly will hear me and be glad. **R.**
Glorify the LORD with me, let us together extol his name. I sought the LORD, and he answered me and delivered me from all my fears. **R.**
Look to him that you may be radiant with joy, and your

faces may not blush with shame. When the poor one called out, the LORD heard, and from all his distress he saved him. **R.**

The angel of the LORD encamps around those who fear him, and delivers them. Taste and see how good the LORD is; blessed the man who takes refuge in him. **R.**

Second Reading: 2 Timothy 4:6-8, 17-18

I, Paul, am already being poured out like a libation, and the time of my departure is at hand. I have competed well; I have finished the race; I have kept the faith. From now on the crown of righteousness awaits me, which the Lord, the just judge, will award to me on that day, and not only to me, but to all who have longed for his appearance. The Lord stood by me and gave me strength, so that through me the proclamation might be completed and all the Gentiles might hear it. And I was rescued from the lion's mouth. The Lord will rescue me from every evil threat and will bring me safe to his heavenly Kingdom. To him be glory forever and ever. Amen.

Alleluia: Matthew 16:18

R. Alleluia, alleluia.

You are Peter and upon this rock I will build my Church, and the gates of the netherworld shall not prevail against it.

R.

Gospel: Matthew 16:13-19

When Jesus went into the region of Caesarea Philippi he asked his disciples, "Who do people say that the Son of Man is?" They replied, "Some say John the Baptist, others Elijah, still others Jeremiah or one of the prophets." He said to them, "But who do you say that I am?" Simon Peter said in reply, "You are the Christ, the Son of the living God." Jesus said to him in reply, "Blessed are you, Simon son of Jonah. For flesh and blood has not revealed this to you, but my heavenly Father. And so I say to you, you are Peter, and upon this rock I will build my Church, and the gates of the netherworld shall not prevail against it. I will give you the keys to the Kingdom of heaven. Whatever you bind on earth shall be bound in heaven; and whatever you loose on earth shall be loosed in heaven."

JULY

SATURDAY, JULY 3

FEAST OF SAINT THOMAS, APOSTLE

First Reading: Ephesians 2:19-22

Brothers and sisters: You are no longer strangers and sojourners, but you are fellow citizens with the holy ones and members of the household of God, built upon the foundation of the Apostles and prophets, with Christ Jesus himself as the capstone. Through him the whole structure is held together and grows into a temple sacred in the Lord; in him you also are being built together into a dwelling place of God in the Spirit.

Responsorial Psalm: Psalm 117:1bc, 2

R. (Mark 16:15) Go out to all the world and tell the Good News.

Praise the LORD, all you nations; glorify him, all you peoples! **R.**

For steadfast is his kindness for us, and the fidelity of the LORD endures forever. **R.**

Alleluia: John 20:29

R. Alleluia, alleluia.

You believe in me, Thomas, because you have seen me, says the Lord; blessed are those who have not seen, but still believe! **R.**

Gospel: John 20:24-29

Thomas, called Didymus, one of the Twelve, was not with them when Jesus came. So the other disciples said to him, "We have seen the Lord." But Thomas said to them, "Unless I see the mark of the nails in his hands and put my finger into the nailmarks and put my hand into his side, I will not believe." Now a week later his disciples were again inside and Thomas was with them. Jesus came, although the doors were locked, and stood in their midst and said, "Peace be with you." Then he said to Thomas, "Put your finger here and see my hands, and bring your hand and put it into my side, and do not be unbelieving, but believe." Thomas answered and said to him, "My Lord and my God!" Jesus said to him, "Have you come to believe because you have seen me? Blessed are those who have not seen and have believed."

FOURTEENTH SUNDAY IN ORDINARY TIME

First Reading: Ezekiel 2:2-5

As the LORD spoke to me, the spirit entered into me and set me on my feet, and I heard the one who was speaking say to me: Son of man, I am sending you to the Israelites, rebels who have rebelled against me; they and their ancestors have revolted against me to this very day. Hard of face and obstinate of heart are they to whom I am sending you. But you shall say to them: Thus says the LORD GOD! And whether they heed or resist— for they are a rebellious house— they shall know that a prophet has been among them.

Responsorial Psalm: Psalm 123:1-2, 2, 3-4

R. (2cd) Our eyes are fixed on the Lord, pleading for his mercy.

To you I lift up my eyes who are enthroned in heaven — as the eyes of servants are on the hands of their masters. **R.**

As the eyes of a maid are on the hands of her mistress, so are our eyes on the LORD, our God, till he have pity on us. **R.**

Have pity on us, O LORD, have pity on us, for we are more than sated with contempt; our souls are more than sated with the mockery of the arrogant, with the contempt of the proud. **R.**

Second Reading: 2 Corinthians 12:7-10

Brothers and sisters: That I, Paul, might not become too elated, because of the abundance of the revelations, a thorn in the flesh was given to me, an angel of Satan, to beat me, to keep me from being too elated. Three times I begged the Lord about this, that it might leave me, but he said to me, "My grace is sufficient for you, for power is made perfect in weakness." I will rather boast most gladly of my weaknesses, in order that the power of Christ may dwell with me. Therefore, I am content with weaknesses, insults, hardships, persecutions, and constraints, for the sake of Christ; for when I am weak, then I am strong.

Alleluia: Luke 4:18
R. Alleluia, alleluia.
The Spirit of the Lord is upon me, for he sent me to bring glad tidings to the poor. **R.**

Gospel: Mark 6:1-6
Jesus departed from there and came to his native place, accompanied by his disciples. When the Sabbath came he

began to teach in the synagogue, and many who heard him were astonished. They said, "Where did this man get all this? What kind of wisdom has been given him? What mighty deeds are wrought by his hands! Is he not the carpenter, the son of Mary, and the brother of James and Joses and Judas and Simon? And are not his sisters here with us?" And they took offense at him. Jesus said to them, "A prophet is not without honor except in his native place and among his own kin and in his own house." So he was not able to perform any mighty deed there, apart from curing a few sick people by laying his hands on them. He was amazed at their lack of faith.

SUNDAY, JULY 11
FIFTEENTH SUNDAY IN ORDINARY TIME
First Reading: Amos 7:12-15

Amaziah, priest of Bethel, said to Amos, "Off with you, visionary, flee to the land of Judah! There earn your bread by prophesying, but never again prophesy in Bethel; for it is the king's sanctuary and a royal temple." Amos answered Amaziah, "I was no prophet, nor have I belonged to a company of prophets; I was a shepherd and a dresser of sycamores. The LORD took me from following the flock, and said to me, Go, prophesy to my people Israel."

Responsorial Psalm: Psalm 85:9-10, 11-12, 13-14

R. (8) Lord, let us see your kindness, and grant us your salvation.

I will hear what God proclaims; the LORD —for he proclaims peace. Near indeed is his salvation to those who fear him, glory dwelling in our land. **R.**

Kindness and truth shall meet; justice and peace shall kiss. Truth shall spring out of the earth, and justice shall look down from heaven. **R.**

The LORD himself will give his benefits; our land shall yield its increase. Justice shall walk before him, and prepare the way of his steps. **R.**

Second Reading: Ephesians 1:3-14 or 1:3-10

Blessed be the God and Father of our Lord Jesus Christ, who has blessed us in Christ with every spiritual blessing in the heavens, as he chose us in him, before the foundation of the world, to be holy and without blemish before him. In love he destined us for adoption to himself through Jesus Christ, in accord with the favor of his will, for the praise of the glory of his grace that he granted us in the beloved. In him we have redemption by his blood, the forgiveness of transgressions, in accord with the riches of his grace that he lavished upon us. In all wisdom and insight, he has made known to us the mystery of his will in accord with his favor that he set forth in him as a plan for the fullness of times, to sum up all things in Christ, in heaven and on earth. In him we were also chosen, destined in accord with the purpose of the One who accomplishes all things according to the intention of his will, so that we might exist for the praise of his glory, we who first hoped in Christ. In him you also, who have heard the word of truth, the gospel of your salvation, and have believed in him, were sealed with the promised holy Spirit, which is the first installment of our inheritance toward redemption as God's possession, to the praise of his glory.

Or:

Ephesians 1:3-10

Blessed be the God and Father of our Lord Jesus Christ, who has blessed us in Christ with every spiritual blessing in the heavens, as he chose us in him, before the foundation of the world, to be holy and without blemish before him. In love he destined us for adoption to himself through Jesus Christ, in accord with the favor of his will, for the praise of the glory of God's grace that he granted us in the beloved. In him we have redemption by his blood, the forgiveness of transgressions, in accord with the riches of his grace that he lavished upon us. In all wisdom and insight, he has made known to us the mystery of his will in accord with his favor that he set forth in him as a plan for the fullness of times, to sum up all things in Christ, in heaven and on earth.

Alleluia: Ephesians 1:17-18

R. Alleluia, alleluia.

May the Father of our Lord Jesus Christ enlighten the eyes of our hearts, that we may know what is the hope that belongs to our call. **R.**

Gospel: Mark 6:7-13

Jesus summoned the Twelve and began to send them out two by two and gave them authority over unclean spirits. He instructed them to take nothing for the journey but a walking stick— no food, no sack, no money in their belts. They were, however, to wear sandals but not a second tunic. He said to them, "Wherever you enter a house, stay there until you leave. Whatever place does not welcome you or listen to you, leave there and shake the dust off your feet in testimony against them." So they went off and preached repentance. The Twelve drove out many demons, and they anointed with oil many who were sick and cured them.

SUNDAY, JULY 18

SIXTEENTH SUNDAY IN ORDINARY TIME

First Reading: Jeremiah 23:1-6

Woe to the shepherds who mislead and scatter the flock of my pasture, says the LORD. Therefore, thus says the LORD, the God of Israel, against the shepherds who shepherd my people: You have scattered my sheep and driven them away. You have not cared for them, but I will take care to punish your evil deeds. I myself will gather the remnant of my flock from all the lands to which I have driven them and bring them back to their meadow; there they shall increase and multiply. I will appoint shepherds for them who will shepherd them so that they need no longer fear and tremble; and none shall be missing, says the LORD. Behold, the days are coming, says the LORD, when I will raise up a righteous shoot to David; as king he shall reign and govern wisely, he shall do what is just and right in the land. In his days Judah shall be saved, Israel shall dwell in security. This is the name they give him: the LORD our justice."

Responsorial Psalm: Psalm 23:1-3, 3-4, 5, 6

R. (1) The Lord is my shepherd; there is nothing I shall want.

The LORD is my shepherd; I shall not want. In verdant pastures he gives me repose; beside restful waters he leads me; he refreshes my soul. **R.**

He guides me in right paths for his name's sake. Even though I walk in the dark valley I fear no evil; for you are at my side with your rod and your staff that give me courage. **R.**

You spread the table before me in the sight of my foes; you anoint my head with oil; my cup overflows. **R.**

Only goodness and kindness follow me all the days of my life; and I shall dwell in the house of the LORD for years to come. **R.**

Second Reading: Ephesians 2:13-18

Brothers and sisters: In Christ Jesus you who once were far off have become near by the blood of Christ. For he is our peace, he who made both one and broke down the dividing wall of enmity, through his flesh, abolishing the law with its commandments and legal claims, that he might create in himself one new person in place of the two, thus establishing peace, and might reconcile both with God, in one body, through the cross, putting that enmity to death by it. He came and preached peace to you who were far off and peace to those who were near, for through him we both have access in one Spirit to the Father.

Alleluia: John 10:27

R. Alleluia, alleluia.

My sheep hear my voice, says the Lord; I know them, and they follow me. **R.**

Gospel: Mark 6:30-34

The apostles gathered together with Jesus and reported all they had done and taught. He said to them, "Come away by yourselves to a deserted place and rest a while." People were coming and going in great numbers, and they had no opportunity even to eat. So they went off in the boat by themselves to a deserted place. People saw them leaving and many came to know about it. They hastened there on foot from all the towns and arrived at the place before them. When he disembarked and saw the vast crowd, his heart was moved with pity for them, for they were like sheep without a shepherd; and he began to teach them many things.

THURSDAY, JULY 22

FEAST OF SAINT MARY MAGDALENE

First Reading: Song of Songs 3:1-4b

The Bride says: On my bed at night I sought him whom my heart loves–I sought him but I did not find him. I will rise then and go about the city; in the streets and crossings I will seek Him whom my heart loves. I sought him but I did not find him. The watchmen came upon me, as they made their rounds of the city: Have you seen him whom my heart loves? I had hardly left them when I found him whom my heart loves.

Or:

2 Corinthians 5:14-17

Brothers and sisters: The love of Christ impels us, once we have come to the conviction that one died for all; therefore, all have died. He indeed died for all, so that those who live might no longer live for themselves but for him who for their sake died and was raised. Consequently, from now on we regard no one according to the flesh; even if we once knew Christ according to the flesh, yet now we know him so no longer. So whoever is in Christ is a new creation: the old things have passed away; behold, new things have come.

Responsorial Psalm: Psalm 63:2, 3-4, 5-6, 8-9

R. (2) My soul is thirsting for you, O Lord my God.

O God, you are my God whom I seek; for you my flesh pines and my soul thirsts like the earth, parched, lifeless and without water. **R.**

Thus have I gazed toward you in the sanctuary to see your power and your glory, for your kindness is a greater good than life; my lips shall glorify you. **R.**

Thus will I bless you while I live; lifting up my hands, I will call upon your name. As with the riches of a banquet shall my soul be satisfied, and with exultant lips my mouth shall praise you. **R.**

You are my help, and in the shadow of your wings I shout for joy. My soul clings fast to you; your right hand upholds me. **R.**

Alleluia

R. Alleluia, alleluia.

Tell us Mary, what did you see on the way? I saw the glory of the risen Christ, I saw his empty tomb. **R.**

Gospel: John 20:1-2, 11-18

On the first day of the week, Mary Magdalene came to the tomb early in the morning, while it was still dark, and saw the stone removed from the tomb. So she ran and went to Simon Peter and to the other disciple whom Jesus loved, and told them, "They have taken the Lord from the tomb, and we don't know where they put him." Mary stayed outside the tomb weeping. And as she wept, she bent over into the tomb and saw two angels in white sitting there, one at the head and one at the feet where the Body of Jesus had been. And they said to her, "Woman, why are you weeping?" She said to them, "They have taken my Lord, and I don't know where they laid him." When she had said this, she turned around and saw Jesus there, but did not know it was Jesus. Jesus said to her, "Woman, why are you weeping? Whom are you looking for?" She thought it was the gardener and said to him, "Sir, if you carried him away, tell me where you laid him, and I will take him." Jesus said to her, "Mary!" She turned and said to him in Hebrew, "Rabbouni," which means Teacher. Jesus said to her, "Stop holding on to me, for I have not yet ascended to the Father. But go to my brothers and tell them, 'I am going to my Father and your Father, to my God and your God.'" Mary Magdalene went and announced to the disciples, "I have seen the Lord," and then reported what he told her.

SUNDAY, JULY 25

SEVENTEENTH SUNDAY IN ORDINARY TIME

First Reading: 2 Kings 4:42-44

A man came from Baal-shalishah bringing to Elisha, the man of God, twenty barley loaves made from the firstfruits, and fresh grain in the ear. Elisha said, "Give it to the people to eat." But his servant objected, "How can I set this before a hundred people?" Elisha insisted, "Give it to the people to eat." "For thus says the LORD, 'They shall eat and there shall be some left over.'" And when they had eaten, there was some left over, as the LORD had said.

Responsorial Psalm: Psalm 145:10-11, 15-16, 17-18

R. (16) The hand of the Lord feeds us; he answers all our needs.

Let all your works give you thanks, O LORD, and let your faithful ones bless you. Let them discourse of the glory of your kingdom and speak of your might. **R.**

The eyes of all look hopefully to you, and you give them their food in due season; you open your hand and satisfy the desire of every living thing. **R.**

The LORD is just in all his ways and holy in all his works. The LORD is near to all who call upon him, to all who call upon him in truth. **R.**

Second Reading: Ephesians 4:1-6

Brothers and sisters: I, a prisoner for the Lord, urge you to live in a manner worthy of the call you have received, with all humility and gentleness, with patience, bearing with one another through love, striving to preserve the unity of the spirit through the bond of peace: one body and one Spirit, as you were also called to the one hope of your call; one Lord, one faith, one baptism; one God and Father of all, who is over all and through all and in all.

Alleluia: Luke 7:16

R. Alleluia, alleluia.

A great prophet has risen in our midst. God has visited his people. **R.**

Gospel: John 6:1-15

Jesus went across the Sea of Galilee. A large crowd followed him, because they saw the signs he was performing on the sick. Jesus went up on the mountain, and there he sat down with his disciples. The Jewish feast of Passover was near. When Jesus raised his eyes and saw that a large crowd was coming to him, he said to Philip, "Where can we buy enough food for them to eat?" He said this to test him, because he himself knew what he was going to do. Philip answered him, "Two hundred days' wages worth of food would not be enough for each of them to have a little." One of his disciples, Andrew, the brother of Simon Peter, said to him, "There is a boy here who has five barley loaves and two fish; but what good are these for so many?" Jesus said, "Have the people recline." Now there was a great deal of grass in that place. So the men reclined, about five thousand in number. Then Jesus took the loaves, gave thanks, and distributed them to those who were reclining, and also as much of the fish as they wanted. When they had had their fill, he said to his disciples, "Gather the fragments left over, so that nothing will be wasted." So they collected them, and filled twelve wicker baskets with fragments from the five barley loaves that had been more than they could eat. When the people saw the sign he had done, they said, "This is truly the Prophet, the one who is to come into the world." Since Jesus knew that they were going to come and carry him off to make him king, he withdrew again to the mountain alone.

AUGUST

SUNDAY, AUGUST 1

EIGHTEENTH SUNDAY IN ORDINARY TIME

First Reading: Exodus 16:2-4, 12-15

The whole Israelite community grumbled against Moses and Aaron. The Israelites said to them, "Would that we had died at the LORD's hand in the land of Egypt, as we sat by our fleshpots and ate our fill of bread! But you had to lead us into this desert to make the whole community die of famine!" Then the LORD said to Moses, "I will now rain down bread from heaven for you. Each day the people are to go out and gather their daily portion; thus will I test them, to see whether they follow my instructions or not. "I have heard the grumbling of the Israelites. Tell them: In the evening twilight you shall eat flesh, and in the morning you shall have your fill of bread, so that you may know that I, the LORD, am your God." In the evening quail came up and covered the camp. In the morning a dew lay all about the camp, and when the dew evaporated, there on the surface of the desert were fine flakes like hoarfrost on the ground. On seeing it, the Israelites asked one another, "What is this?" for they did not know what it was. But Moses told them, "This is the bread that the LORD has given you to eat."

Responsorial Psalm: Psalm 78:3-4, 23-24, 25, 54

R. (24b) The Lord gave them bread from heaven.

What we have heard and know, and what our fathers have declared to us, we will declare to the generation to come the glorious deeds of the LORD and his strength and the wonders that he wrought. **R.**

He commanded the skies above and opened the doors of heaven; he rained manna upon them for food and gave them heavenly bread. **R.**

Man ate the bread of angels, food he sent them in abundance. And he brought them to his holy land, to the mountains his right hand had won. **R.**

Second Reading: Ephesians 4:17, 20-24

Brothers and sisters: I declare and testify in the Lord that you must no longer live as the Gentiles do, in the futility of their minds; that is not how you learned Christ, assuming that you have heard of him and were taught in him, as truth is in Jesus, that you should put away the old self of your former way of life, corrupted through deceitful desires, and be renewed in the spirit of your minds, and put on the new self, created in God's way in righteousness and holiness of truth.

Alleluia: Matthew 4:4b

R. Alleluia, alleluia.

One does not live on bread alone, but on every word that comes forth from the mouth of God. **R.**

Gospel: John 6:24-35

When the crowd saw that neither Jesus nor his disciples were there, they themselves got into boats and came to Capernaum looking for Jesus. And when they found him across the sea they said to him, "Rabbi, when did you get here?" Jesus answered them and said, "Amen, amen, I say to you, you are looking for me not because you saw signs but because you ate the loaves and were filled. Do not work for food that perishes but for the food that endures for eternal life, which the Son of Man will give you. For on him the Father, God, has set his seal." So they said to him, "What can we do to accomplish the works of God?" Jesus answered and said to them, "This is the work of God, that you believe in the one he sent." So they said to him, "What sign can you do, that we may see and believe in you? What can you do? Our ancestors ate manna in the desert, as it is written: *He gave them bread from heaven to eat.*" So Jesus said to them, "Amen, amen, I say to you, it was not Moses who gave the bread from heaven; my Father gives you the true bread from heaven. For the bread of God is that which comes down from heaven and gives life to the world." So they said to him, "Sir, give us this bread always." Jesus said to them, "I am the bread of life; whoever comes to me will never hunger, and whoever believes in me will never thirst."

FRIDAY, AUGUST 6
FEAST OF THE TRANSFIGURATION OF THE LORD
First Reading: Daniel 7:9-10, 13-14

As I watched: Thrones were set up and the Ancient One took his throne. His clothing was bright as snow, and the hair on his head as white as wool; his throne was flames of fire, with wheels of burning fire. A surging stream of fire flowed out from where he sat; Thousands upon thousands were ministering to him, and myriads upon myriads attended him. The court was convened and the books were opened. As the visions during the night continued, I saw: One like a Son of man coming, on the clouds of heaven; when he reached the Ancient One and was presented before him, the one like a Son of man received dominion, glory, and kingship; all peoples, nations, and languages serve him. His dominion is an everlasting dominion that shall not be taken away, his kingship shall not be destroyed.

Responsorial Psalm: Psalm 97:1-2, 5-6, 9

R. (1a and 9a) The Lord is king, the Most High over all the earth.

The LORD is king; let the earth rejoice; let the many islands be glad. Clouds and darkness are round about him, justice and judgment are the foundation of his throne. **R.**

The mountains melt like wax before the LORD, before the LORD of all the earth. The heavens proclaim his justice, and all peoples see his glory. **R.**

Because you, O LORD, are the Most High over all the earth, exalted far above all gods. **R.**

Second Reading: 2 Peter 1:16-19

Beloved: We did not follow cleverly devised myths when we made known to you the power and coming of our Lord Jesus Christ, but we had been eyewitnesses of his majesty. For he received honor and glory from God the Father when that unique declaration came to him from the majestic glory, "This is my Son, my beloved, with whom I am well pleased." We ourselves heard this voice come from heaven while we were with him on the holy mountain. Moreover, we possess the prophetic message that is altogether reliable. You will do well to be attentive to it, as to a lamp shining in a dark place, until day dawns and the morning star rises in your hearts.

Alleluia: Matthew 17:5c
R. Alleluia, alleluia.

This is my beloved Son, with whom I am well pleased; listen to him. **R.**

Gospel: Mark 9:2-10

Jesus took Peter, James, and his brother John, and led them up a high mountain apart by themselves. And he was transfigured before them, and his clothes became dazzling white, such as no fuller on earth could bleach them. Then Elijah appeared to them along with Moses, and they were conversing with Jesus. Then Peter said to Jesus in reply, "Rabbi, it is good that we are here! Let us make three tents: one for you, one for Moses, and one for Elijah." He hardly knew what to say, they were so terrified. Then a cloud came, casting a shadow over them; from the cloud came a voice, "This is my beloved Son. Listen to him." Suddenly, looking around, they no longer saw anyone but Jesus alone with them. As they were coming down from the mountain, he charged them not to relate what they had seen to anyone, except when the Son of Man had risen from the dead. So they kept the matter to themselves, questioning what rising from the dead meant.

SUNDAY, AUGUST 8
NINETEENTH SUNDAY IN ORDINARY TIME
First Reading: 1 Kings 19:4-8

Elijah went a day's journey into the desert, until he came to a broom tree and sat beneath it. He prayed for death saying: "This is enough, O LORD! Take my life, for I am no better than my fathers." He lay down and fell asleep under the broom tree, but then an angel touched him and ordered him to get up and eat. Elijah looked and there at his head was a hearth cake and a jug of water. After he ate and drank, he lay down again, but the angel of the LORD came back a second time, touched him, and ordered, "Get up and eat, else the journey will be too long for you!" He got up, ate, and drank; then strengthened by that food, he walked forty days and forty nights to the mountain of God, Horeb.

Responsorial Psalm: Psalm 34:2-3, 4-5, 6-7, 8-9
R. (9a) Taste and see the goodness of the Lord.

I will bless the LORD at all times; his praise shall be ever in my mouth. Let my soul glory in the LORD; the lowly will hear me and be glad. **R.**

Glorify the LORD with me, Let us together extol his name. I sought the LORD, and he answered me and delivered me from all my fears. **R.**

Look to him that you may be radiant with joy. And your faces may not blush with shame. When the afflicted man called out, the LORD heard, and from all his distress he saved him. **R.**

The angel of the LORD encamps around those who fear him and delivers them. Taste and see how good the LORD is; blessed the man who takes refuge in him. **R.**

Second Reading: Ephesians 4:30-5:2

Brothers and sisters: Do not grieve the Holy Spirit of God, with which you were sealed for the day of redemption. All bitterness, fury, anger, shouting, and reviling must be removed from you, along with all malice. And be kind to one another, compassionate, forgiving one another as God has forgiven you in Christ. So be imitators of God, as beloved children, and live in love, as Christ loved us and handed himself over for us as a sacrificial offering to God for a fragrant aroma.

Alleluia: John 6:51
R. Alleluia, alleluia.

I am the living bread that came down from heaven, says the Lord; whoever eats this bread will live forever. **R**.

Gospel: John 6:41-51

The Jews murmured about Jesus because he said, "I am the bread that came down from heaven," and they said, "Is this not Jesus, the son of Joseph? Do we not know his father and mother? Then how can he say, 'I have come down from heaven'?" Jesus answered and said to them, "Stop murmuring among yourselves. No one can come to me unless the Father who sent me draw him, and I will raise him on the last day. It is written in the prophets: *They shall all be taught by God.* Everyone who listens to my Father and learns from him comes to me. Not that anyone has seen the Father except the one who is from God; he has seen the Father. Amen, amen, I say to you, whoever believes has eternal life. I am the bread of life. Your ancestors ate the manna in the desert, but they died; this is the bread that comes down from heaven so that one may eat it and not die. I am the living bread that came down from heaven; whoever eats this bread will live forever; and the bread that I will give is my flesh for the life of the world."

TUESDAY, AUGUST 10

FEAST OF SAINT LAWRENCE, DEACON AND MARTYR

First Reading: 2 Corinthians 9:6-10

Brothers and sisters: Whoever sows sparingly will also reap sparingly, and whoever sows bountifully will also reap bountifully. Each must do as already determined, without sadness or compulsion, for God loves a cheerful giver. Moreover, God is able to make every grace abundant for you, so that in all things, always having all you need, you may have an abundance for every good work. As it is written: *He scatters abroad, he gives to the poor; his righteousness endures forever.* The one who supplies seed to the sower and bread for food will supply and multiply your seed and increase the harvest of your righteousness.

Responsorial Psalm: Psalm 112:1-2, 5-6, 7-8, 9

R. (5) Blessed the man who is gracious and lends to those in need.

Blessed the man who fears the LORD, who greatly delights in his commands. His posterity shall be mighty upon the earth; the upright generation shall be blessed. **R.**

Well for the man who is gracious and lends, who conducts his affairs with justice; He shall never be moved; the just one shall be in everlasting remembrance. **R.**

An evil report he shall not fear; his heart is firm, trusting in the LORD. His heart is steadfast; he shall not fear till he looks down upon his foes. **R.**

Lavishly he gives to the poor, his generosity shall endure forever; his horn shall be exalted in glory. **R.**

Alleluia: John 8:12bc

R. Alleluia, alleluia.

Whoever follows me will not walk in darkness but will have the light of life, says the Lord. **R.**

Gospel: John 12:24-26

Jesus said to his disciples: "Amen, amen, I say to you, unless a grain of wheat falls to the ground and dies, it remains just a grain of wheat; but if it dies, it produces much fruit. Whoever loves his life loses it, and whoever hates his life in this world will preserve it for eternal life. Whoever serves me must follow me, and where I am, there also will my servant be. The Father will honor whoever serves me."

SUNDAY, AUGUST 15

SOLEMNITY OF THE ASSUMPTION OF THE BLESSED VIRGIN MARY

(Vigil Mass)

First Reading: 1 Chronicles 15:3-4, 15-16; 16:1-2

David assembled all Israel in Jerusalem to bring the ark of the Lord to the place which he had prepared for it. David also called together the sons of Aaron and the Levites. The Levites bore the ark of God on their shoulders with poles, as Moses had ordained according to the word of the Lord. David commanded the chiefs of the Levites to appoint their kinsmen as chanters, to play on musical instruments, harps, lyres, and cymbals, to make a loud sound of rejoicing. They brought in the ark of God and set it within the tent which David had pitched for it. Then they offered up burnt offerings and peace offerings to God. When David had finished offering up the burnt offerings and peace offerings, he blessed the people in the name of the Lord.

Responsorial Psalm: Psalm 132:6-7, 9-10, 13-14

R. (8) Lord, go up to the place of your rest, you and the ark of your holiness.

Behold, we heard of it in Ephrathah; we found it in the fields of Jaar. Let us enter his dwelling, let us worship at his footstool. **R.**

May your priests be clothed with justice; let your faithful ones shout merrily for joy. For the sake of David your servant, reject not the plea of your anointed. **R.**

For the LORD has chosen Zion; he prefers her for his dwelling. "Zion is my resting place forever; in her will I dwell, for I prefer her." **R.**

Second Reading: 1 Corinthians 15:54b-57

Brothers and sisters: When that which is mortal clothes itself with immortality, then the word that is written shall come about: *Death is swallowed up in victory. Where, O death, is your victory? Where, O death, is your sting?* The sting of death is sin, and the power of sin is the law. But thanks be to God who gives us the victory through our Lord Jesus Christ.

Alleluia: Luke 11:28

R. Alleluia, alleluia.

Blessed are they who hear the word of God and observe it.

R.

Gospel: Luke 11:27-28

While Jesus was speaking, a woman from the crowd called out and said to him, "Blessed is the womb that carried you and the breasts at which you nursed." He replied, "Rather, blessed are those who hear the word of God and observe it."

SOLEMNITY OF THE ASSUMPTION OF THE BLESSED VIRGIN MARY

(Mass during the Day)

First Reading: Revelation 11:19a; 12:1-6a, 10ab

God's temple in heaven was opened, and the ark of his covenant could be seen in the temple. A great sign appeared in the sky, a woman clothed with the sun, with the moon under her feet, and on her head a crown of twelve stars. She was with child and wailed aloud in pain as she labored to give birth. Then another sign appeared in the sky; it was a huge red dragon, with seven heads and ten horns, and on its heads were seven diadems. Its tail swept away a third of the stars in the sky and hurled them down to the earth. Then the dragon stood before the woman about to give birth, to devour her child when she gave birth. She gave birth to a son, a male child, destined to rule all the nations with an iron rod. Her child was caught up to God and his throne. The woman herself fled into the desert where she had a place prepared by God. Then I heard a loud voice in heaven say: "Now have salvation and power come, and the

Kingdom of our God and the authority of his Anointed One."

Responsorial Psalm: Psalm 45:10, 11, 12, 16
R. (10bc) The queen stands at your right hand, arrayed in gold.
The queen takes her place at your right hand in gold of Ophir. **R.**
Hear, O daughter, and see; turn your ear, forget your people and your father's house. **R.**
So shall the king desire your beauty; for he is your lord. **R.**
They are borne in with gladness and joy; they enter the palace of the king. **R.**

Second Reading: 1 Corinthians 15:20-27
Brothers and sisters: Christ has been raised from the dead, the firstfruits of those who have fallen asleep. For since death came through man, the resurrection of the dead came also through man. For just as in Adam all die, so too in Christ shall all be brought to life, but each one in proper order: Christ the firstfruits; then, at his coming, those who belong to Christ; then comes the end, when he hands over the Kingdom to his God and Father, when he has destroyed every sovereignty and every authority and power. For he

must reign until he has put all his enemies under his feet. The last enemy to be destroyed is death, for "he subjected everything under his feet."

Alleluia

R. Alleluia, alleluia.

Mary is taken up to heaven; a chorus of angels exults. **R.**

Gospel: Luke 1:39-56

Mary set out and traveled to the hill country in haste to a town of Judah, where she entered the house of Zechariah and greeted Elizabeth. When Elizabeth heard Mary's greeting, the infant leaped in her womb, and Elizabeth, filled with the Holy Spirit, cried out in a loud voice and said, "Blessed are you among women, and blessed is the fruit of your womb. And how does this happen to me, that the mother of my Lord should come to me? For at the moment the sound of your greeting reached my ears, the infant in my womb leaped for joy. Blessed are you who believed that what was spoken to you by the Lord would be fulfilled." And Mary said: "My soul proclaims the greatness of the Lord; my spirit rejoices in God my Savior for he has looked with favor on his lowly servant. From this day all generations will call me blessed: the Almighty has done great things for me and holy is his Name. He has mercy on those who fear him in every generation. He has shown the strength of his arm, and has scattered the proud in their conceit. He has cast down the mighty from their thrones, and has lifted up the lowly. He has filled the hungry with good things, and the rich he has sent away empty. He has come to the help of his servant Israel for he has remembered his promise of mercy, the promise he made to our fathers, to Abraham and his children forever." Mary remained with her about three months and then returned to her home.

SUNDAY, AUGUST 22
TWENTY-FIRST SUNDAY IN ORDINARY TIME
First Reading: Joshua 24:1-2a, 15-17, 18b

Joshua gathered together all the tribes of Israel at Shechem, summoning their elders, their leaders, their judges, and their officers. When they stood in ranks before God, Joshua addressed all the people: "If it does not please you to serve the LORD, decide today whom you will serve, the gods your fathers served beyond the River or the gods of the Amorites in whose country you are now dwelling. As for me and my household, we will serve the LORD." But the people answered, "Far be it from us to forsake the LORD for the service of other gods. For it was the LORD, our God, who brought us and our fathers up out of the land of Egypt, out of a state of slavery. He performed those great miracles before our very eyes and protected us along our entire journey and among the peoples through whom we passed. Therefore we also will serve the LORD, for he is our God."

Responsorial Psalm: Psalm 34:2-3, 16-17, 18-19, 20-21
R. (9a) Taste and see the goodness of the Lord.
I will bless the LORD at all times; his praise shall be ever in my mouth. Let my soul glory in the LORD; the lowly will hear me and be glad. **R.**
The LORD has eyes for the just, and ears for their cry. The LORD confronts the evildoers, to destroy remembrance of them from the earth. **R.**
When the just cry out, the LORD hears them, and from all their distress he rescues them. The LORD is close to the brokenhearted; and those who are crushed in spirit he saves. **R.**
Many are the troubles of the just one, but out of them all the LORD delivers him; he watches over all his bones; not one of them shall be broken. **R.**

Second Reading: Ephesians 5:21-32 or 5:2a, 25-32

Brothers and sisters: Be subordinate to one another out of reverence for Christ. Wives should be subordinate to their husbands as to the Lord. For the husband is head of his wife just as Christ is head of the church, he himself the savior of the body. As the church is subordinate to Christ, so wives should be subordinate to their husbands in everything. Husbands, love your wives, even as Christ loved the church and handed himself over for her to sanctify her, cleansing her by the bath of water with the word, that he might present to himself the church in splendor, without spot or wrinkle or any such thing, that she might be holy and without blemish. So also husbands should love their wives as their own bodies. He who loves his wife loves himself. For no one hates his own flesh but rather nourishes and cherishes it, even as Christ does the church, because we are members of his body. *For this reason a man shall leave his father and his mother and be joined to his wife, and the two shall become one flesh.* This is a great mystery, but I speak in reference to Christ and the church.

Or:
Ephesians 5:2a, 25-32
Brothers and sisters: Live in love, as Christ loved us. Husbands, love your wives, even as Christ loved the church

and handed himself over for her to sanctify her, cleansing her by the bath of water with the word, that he might present to himself the church in splendor, without spot or wrinkle or any such thing, that she might be holy and without blemish. So also husbands should love their wives as their own bodies. He who loves his wife loves himself. For no one hates his own flesh but rather nourishes and cherishes it, even as Christ does the church, because we are members of his body. *For this reason a man shall leave his father and his mother and be joined to his wife, and the two shall become one flesh.* This is a great mystery, but I speak in reference to Christ and the church.

Alleluia: John 6:63c, 68c
R. Alleluia, alleluia.

Your words, Lord, are Spirit and life; you have the words of everlasting life. **R.**

Gospel: John 6:60-69

Many of Jesus' disciples who were listening said, "This saying is hard; who can accept it?" Since Jesus knew that his disciples were murmuring about this, he said to them, "Does this shock you? What if you were to see the Son of Man ascending to where he was before? It is the spirit that gives life, while the flesh is of no avail. The words I have spoken to you are Spirit and life. But there are some of you who do not believe." Jesus knew from the beginning the ones who would not believe and the one who would betray him. And he said, "For this reason I have told you that no one can come to me unless it is granted him by my Father." As a result of this, many of his disciples returned to their former way of life and no longer accompanied him. Jesus then said to the Twelve, "Do you also want to leave?" Simon Peter answered him, "Master, to whom shall we go? You have the words of eternal life. We have come to believe and are convinced that you are the Holy One of God."

TUESDAY, AUGUST 24
FEAST OF SAINT BARTHOLOMEW, APOSTLE
First Reading: Revelation 21:9b-14

The angel spoke to me, saying, "Come here. I will show you the bride, the wife of the Lamb." He took me in spirit to a great, high mountain and showed me the holy city Jerusalem coming down out of heaven from God. It gleamed with the splendor of God. Its radiance was like that of a precious stone, like jasper, clear as crystal. It had a massive, high wall, with twelve gates where twelve angels were stationed and on which names were inscribed, the names of the twelve tribes of the children of Israel. There were three gates facing east, three north, three south, and three west. The wall of the city had twelve courses of stones as its foundation, on which were inscribed the twelve names of the twelve Apostles of the Lamb.

Responsorial Psalm: Psalm 145:10-11, 12-13, 17-18
R. (12) Your friends make known, O Lord, the glorious splendor of your Kingdom.
Let all your works give you thanks, O LORD, and let your faithful ones bless you. Let them discourse of the glory of your Kingdom and speak of your might. **R.**
Making known to men your might and the glorious splendor of your Kingdom. Your Kingdom is a Kingdom for all ages, and your dominion endures through all generations. **R.**
The LORD is just in all his ways and holy in all his works. The LORD is near to all who call upon him, to all who call upon him in truth. **R.**

Alleluia: John 1:49b
R. Alleluia, alleluia.
Rabbi, you are the Son of God; you are the King of Israel. **R.**

Gospel: John 1:45-51

Philip found Nathanael and told him, "We have found the one about whom Moses wrote in the law, and also the prophets, Jesus son of Joseph, from Nazareth." But Nathanael said to him, "Can anything good come from Nazareth?" Philip said to him, "Come and see." Jesus saw Nathanael coming toward him and said of him, "Here is a true child of Israel. There is no duplicity in him." Nathanael said to him, "How do you know me?" Jesus answered and said to him, "Before Philip called you, I saw you under the fig tree." Nathanael answered him, "Rabbi, you are the Son of God; you are the King of Israel." Jesus answered and said to him, "Do you believe because I told you that I saw you under the fig tree? You will see greater things than this." And he said to him, "Amen, amen, I say to you, you will see heaven opened and the angels of God ascending and descending on the Son of Man."

SUNDAY, AUGUST 29
TWENTY-SECOND SUNDAY IN ORDINARY TIME
First Reading: Deuteronomy 4:1-2, 6-8

Moses said to the people: "Now, Israel, hear the statutes and decrees which I am teaching you to observe, that you may live, and may enter in and take possession of the land which the LORD, the God of your fathers, is giving you. In your observance of the commandments of the LORD, your God, which I enjoin upon you, you shall not add to what I command you nor subtract from it. Observe them carefully, for thus will you give evidence of your wisdom and intelligence to the nations, who will hear of all these statutes and say, 'This great nation is truly a wise and intelligent people.' For what great nation is there that has gods so close to it as the LORD, our God, is to us whenever we call upon him? Or what great nation has statutes and decrees that are as just as this whole law which I am setting before you today?"

Responsorial Psalm: Psalm 15:2-3, 3-4, 4-5
R. (1a) One who does justice will live in the presence of the Lord.

Whoever walks blamelessly and does justice; who thinks the truth in his heart and slanders not with his tongue. **R.**
Who harms not his fellow man, nor takes up a reproach against his neighbor; by whom the reprobate is despised, while he honors those who fear the LORD. **R.**
Who lends not his money at usury and accepts no bribe against the innocent. Whoever does these things shall never be disturbed. **R.**

Second Reading: James 1:17-18, 21b-22, 27

Dearest brothers and sisters: All good giving and every perfect gift is from above, coming down from the Father of lights, with whom there is no alteration or shadow caused by change. He willed to give us birth by the word of truth that we may be a kind of firstfruits of his creatures. Humbly welcome the word that has been planted in you and is able to save your souls. Be doers of the word and not hearers only, deluding yourselves. Religion that is pure and undefiled before God and the Father is this: to care for orphans and widows in their affliction and to keep oneself unstained by the world.

Alleluia: James 1:18
R. Alleluia, alleluia.

The Father willed to give us birth by the word of truth that we may be a kind of firstfruits of his creatures. **R.**

Gospel: Mark 7:1-8, 14-15, 21-23

When the Pharisees with some scribes who had come from Jerusalem gathered around Jesus, they observed that some of his disciples ate their meals with unclean, that is, unwashed, hands. — For the Pharisees and, in fact, all Jews, do not eat without carefully washing their hands, keeping the tradition of the elders. And on coming from the marketplace they do not eat without purifying themselves. And there are many other things that they have traditionally observed, the purification of cups and jugs and kettles and beds. —So the Pharisees and scribes questioned him, "Why do your disciples not follow the tradition of the elders but instead eat a meal with unclean hands?" He responded, "Well did Isaiah prophesy about you hypocrites, as it is written: *This people honors me with their lips, but their hearts are far from me; in vain do they worship me, teaching as doctrines human precepts.* You disregard God's commandment but cling to human tradition." He summoned the crowd again and said to them, "Hear me, all of you, and understand. Nothing that enters one from outside can defile that person; but the things that come out from within are what defile. "From within people, from their hearts, come evil thoughts, unchastity, theft, murder, adultery, greed, malice, deceit, licentiousness, envy, blasphemy, arrogance, folly. All these evils come from within and they defile."

SEPTEMBER

TWENTY-THIRD SUNDAY IN ORDINARY TIME

First Reading: Isaiah 35:4-7a

Thus says the LORD: Say to those whose hearts are frightened: Be strong, fear not! Here is your God, he comes with vindication; with divine recompense he comes to save you. Then will the eyes of the blind be opened, the ears of the deaf be cleared; then will the lame leap like a stag, then the tongue of the mute will sing. Streams will burst forth in the desert, and rivers in the steppe. The burning sands will become pools, and the thirsty ground, springs of water.

Responsorial Psalm: Psalm 146:6-7, 8-9, 9-10

R. (1b) Praise the Lord, my soul!

Or:

R. Alleluia.

The God of Jacob keeps faith forever, secures justice for the oppressed, gives food to the hungry. The LORD sets captives free. **R.**

The LORD gives sight to the blind; the LORD raises up those who were bowed down. The LORD loves the just; the LORD protects strangers. **R.**

The fatherless and the widow the LORD sustains, but the way of the wicked he thwarts. The LORD shall reign forever; your God, O Zion, through all generations. Alleluia. **R.**

Second Reading: James 2:1-5

My brothers and sisters, show no partiality as you adhere to the faith in our glorious Lord Jesus Christ. For if a man with gold rings and fine clothes comes into your assembly, and a poor person in shabby clothes also comes in, and you pay attention to the one wearing the fine clothes and say, "Sit here, please," while you say to the poor one, "Stand there," or "Sit at my feet," have you not made distinctions among yourselves and become judges with evil designs? Listen, my beloved brothers and sisters. Did not God choose those who are poor in the world to be rich in faith and heirs of the kingdom that he promised to those who love him?

Alleluia: Matthew 4:23
R. Alleluia, alleluia.
Jesus proclaimed the Gospel of the kingdom and cured every disease among the people. **R.**

Gospel: Mark 7:31-37

Again Jesus left the district of Tyre and went by way of Sidon to the Sea of Galilee, into the district of the Decapolis. And people brought to him a deaf man who had a speech impediment and begged him to lay his hand on him. He took him off by himself away from the crowd. He put his finger into the man's ears and, spitting, touched his tongue; then he looked up to heaven and groaned, and said to him, "*Ephphatha!*" — that is, "Be opened!" — And immediately the man's ears were opened, his speech impediment was removed, and he spoke plainly. He ordered them not to tell anyone. But the more he ordered them not to, the more they proclaimed it. They were exceedingly astonished and they said, "He has done all things well. He makes the deaf hear and the mute speak."

WEDNESDAY, SEPTEMBER 8
FEAST OF THE NATIVITY OF THE BLESSED VIRGIN MARY

First Reading: Micah 5:1-4a or Romans 8:28-30

The LORD says: You, Bethlehem-Ephrathah, too small to be among the clans of Judah, from you shall come forth for me one who is to be ruler in Israel; Whose origin is from of old, from ancient times. (Therefore the Lord will give them up, until the time when she who is to give birth has borne, and the rest of his brethren shall return to the children of Israel.) He shall stand firm and shepherd his flock by the strength of the LORD, in the majestic name of the LORD, his God; and they shall remain, for now his greatness shall reach to the ends of the earth; he shall be peace.

Or:

Romans 8:28-30

Brothers and sisters: We know that all things work for good for those who love God, who are called according to his purpose. For those he foreknew he also predestined to be conformed to the image of his Son, so that he might be the firstborn among many brothers. And those he predestined he also called; and those he called he also justified; and those he justified he also glorified.

Responsorial Psalm: Psalm 13:6ab, 6c

R. (Isaiah 61:10) With delight I rejoice in the Lord.

Though I trusted in your mercy, let my heart rejoice in your salvation. **R.**

Let me sing of the LORD, "He has been good to me." **R.**

Alleluia

R. Alleluia, alleluia.

Blessed are you, holy Virgin Mary, deserving of all praise; from you rose the sun of Justice, Christ our God. **R**.

Gospel: Matthew 1:1-16, 18-23 or 1:18-23

The Book of the genealogy of Jesus Christ, the son of David, the son of Abraham. Abraham became the father of Isaac, Isaac the father of Jacob, Jacob the father of Judah and his brothers. Judah became the father of Perez and Zerah, whose mother was Tamar. Perez became the father of Hezron, Hezron the father of Ram, Ram the father of Amminadab. Amminadab became the father of Nahshon, Nahshon the father of Salmon, Salmon the father of Boaz, whose mother was Rahab. Boaz became the father of Obed, whose mother was Ruth. Obed became the father of Jesse, Jesse the father of David the king. David became the father of Solomon, whose mother had been the wife of Uriah. Solomon became the father of Rehoboam, Rehoboam the father of Abijah, Abijah the father of Asaph. Asaph became the father of Jehoshaphat, Jehoshaphat the father of Joram, Joram the father of Uzziah. Uzziah became the father of Jotham, Jotham the father of Ahaz, Ahaz the father of Hezekiah. Hezekiah became the father of Manasseh, Manasseh the father of Amos, Amos the father of Josiah. Josiah became the father of Jechoniah and his brothers at the time of the

Babylonian exile. After the Babylonian exile, Jechoniah became the father of Shealtiel, Shealtiel the father of Zerubbabel, Zerubbabel the father of Abiud. Abiud became the father of Eliakim, Eliakim the father of Azor, Azor the father of Zadok. Zadok became the father of Achim, Achim the father of Eliud, Eliud the father of Eleazar. Eleazar became the father of Matthan, Matthan the father of Jacob, Jacob the father of Joseph, the husband of Mary. Of her was born Jesus who is called the Christ. Now this is how the birth of Jesus Christ came about. When his mother Mary was betrothed to Joseph, but before they lived together, she was found with child through the Holy Spirit. Joseph her husband, since he was a righteous man, yet unwilling to expose her to shame, decided to divorce her quietly. Such was his intention when, behold, the angel of the Lord appeared to him in a dream and said, "Joseph, son of David, do not be afraid to take Mary your wife into your home. For it is through the Holy Spirit that this child has been conceived in her. She will bear a son and you are to name him Jesus, because he will save his people from their sins." All this took place to fulfill what the Lord had said through the prophet: *Behold, the virgin shall be with child and bear a son, and they shall name him Emmanuel,* which means "God is with us."

Or:

Matthew 1:18-23

This is how the birth of Jesus Christ came about. When his mother Mary was betrothed to Joseph, but before they lived together, she was found with child through the Holy Spirit. Joseph her husband, since he was a righteous man, yet unwilling to expose her to shame, decided to divorce her quietly. Such was his intention when, behold, the angel of the Lord appeared to him in a dream and said, "Joseph, son of David, do not be afraid to take Mary your wife into your home. For it is through the Holy Spirit that this child has been conceived in her. She will bear a son and you are to name him Jesus, because he will save his people from their sins." All this took place to fulfill what the Lord had said through the prophet: *Behold, the virgin shall be with child and bear a son, and they shall name him Emmanuel,* which means "God is with us."

SUNDAY, SEPTEMBER 12

TWENTY-FOURTH SUNDAY IN ORDINARY TIME

First Reading: Isaiah 50:5-9a

The Lord GOD opens my ear that I may hear; and I have not rebelled, have not turned back. I gave my back to those who beat me, my cheeks to those who plucked my beard; my face

I did not shield from buffets and spitting. The Lord GOD is my help, therefore I am not disgraced; I have set my face like flint, knowing that I shall not be put to shame. He is near who upholds my right; if anyone wishes to oppose me, let us appear together. Who disputes my right? Let that man confront me. See, the Lord GOD is my help; who will prove me wrong?

Responsorial Psalm: Psalm 114:1-2, 3-4, 5-6, 8-9
R. (9) I will walk before the Lord, in the land of the living.
Or:
R. Alleluia.
I love the LORD because he has heard my voice in supplication, because he has inclined his ear to me the day I called. **R.**
The cords of death encompassed me; the snares of the netherworld seized upon me; I fell into distress and sorrow, and I called upon the name of the LORD, "O LORD, save my life!" **R.**
Gracious is the LORD and just; yes, our God is merciful. The LORD keeps the little ones; I was brought low, and he saved me. **R.**
For he has freed my soul from death, my eyes from tears, my

feet from stumbling. I shall walk before the Lord in the land of the living. **R.**

Second Reading: James 2:14-18

What good is it, my brothers and sisters, if someone says he has faith but does not have works? Can that faith save him? If a brother or sister has nothing to wear and has no food for the day, and one of you says to them, "Go in peace, keep warm, and eat well," but you do not give them the necessities of the body, what good is it? So also faith of itself, if it does not have works, is dead. Indeed someone might say, "You have faith and I have works." Demonstrate your faith to me without works, and I will demonstrate my faith to you from my works.

Alleluia: Galatians 6:14
R. Alleluia, alleluia.
May I never boast except in the cross of our Lord through which the world has been crucified to me and I to the world. **R.**

Gospel: Mark 8:27-35

Jesus and his disciples set out for the villages of Caesarea Philippi. Along the way he asked his disciples, "Who do people say that I am?" They said in reply, "John the Baptist, others Elijah, still others one of the prophets." And he asked them, "But who do you say that I am?" Peter said to him in reply, "You are the Christ." Then he warned them not to tell anyone about him. He began to teach them that the Son of Man must suffer greatly and be rejected by the elders, the chief priests, and the scribes, and be killed, and rise after three days. He spoke this openly. Then Peter took him aside and began to rebuke him. At this he turned around and, looking at his disciples, rebuked Peter and said, "Get behind me, Satan. You are thinking not as God does, but as human beings do." He summoned the crowd with his disciples and said to them, "Whoever wishes to come after me must deny himself, take up his cross, and follow me. For whoever wishes to save his life will lose it, but whoever loses his life for my sake and that of the gospel will save it."

TUESDAY, SEPTEMBER 14
FEAST OF THE EXALTATION OF THE HOLY CROSS
First Reading: Numbers 21:4b-9

With their patience worn out by the journey, the people complained against God and Moses, "Why have you brought us up from Egypt to die in this desert, where there is no food or water? We are disgusted with this wretched food!" In punishment the LORD sent among the people saraph serpents, which bit the people so that many of them died. Then the people came to Moses and said, "We have sinned in complaining against the LORD and you. Pray the LORD to take the serpents from us." So Moses prayed for the people, and the LORD said to Moses, "Make a saraph and mount it on a pole, and if any who have been bitten look at it, they will live." Moses accordingly made a bronze serpent and mounted it on a pole, and whenever anyone who had been bitten by a serpent looked at the bronze serpent, he lived.

Responsorial Psalm: Psalm 78:1bc-2, 34-35, 36-37, 38
R. (7b) Do not forget the works of the Lord!
Hearken, my people, to my teaching; incline your ears to the words of my mouth. I will open my mouth in a parable, I will utter mysteries from of old. **R.**
While he slew them they sought him and inquired after God again, remembering that God was their rock and the Most High God, their redeemer. **R.**
But they flattered him with their mouths and lied to him with their tongues, though their hearts were not steadfast toward him, nor were they faithful to his covenant. **R.**

But he, being merciful, forgave their sin and destroyed them not; often he turned back his anger and let none of his wrath be roused. **R.**

Second Reading: Philippians 2:6-11

Brothers and sisters: Christ Jesus, though he was in the form of God, did not regard equality with God something to be grasped. Rather, he emptied himself, taking the form of a slave, coming in human likeness; and found human in appearance, he humbled himself, becoming obedient to death, even death on a cross. Because of this, God greatly exalted him and bestowed on him the name that is above every name, that at the name of Jesus every knee should bend, of those in heaven and on earth and under the earth, and every tongue confess that Jesus Christ is Lord, to the glory of God the Father.

Alleluia

R. Alleluia, alleluia.

We adore you, O Christ, and we bless you, because by your Cross you have redeemed the world. **R.**

Gospel: John 3:13-17

Jesus said to Nicodemus: "No one has gone up to heaven except the one who has come down from heaven, the Son of Man. And just as Moses lifted up the serpent in the desert, so must the Son of Man be lifted up, so that everyone who believes in him may have eternal life." For God so loved the world that he gave his only Son, so that everyone who believes in him might not perish but might have eternal life. For God did not send his Son into the world to condemn the world, but that the world might be saved through him.

SUNDAY, SEPTEMBER 19
TWENTY-FIFTH SUNDAY IN ORDINARY TIME
First Reading: Wisdom 2:12, 17-20

The wicked say: Let us beset the just one, because he is obnoxious to us; he sets himself against our doings, reproaches us for transgressions of the law and charges us with violations of our training. Let us see whether his words be true; let us find out what will happen to him. For if the just one be the son of God, God will defend him and deliver him from the hand of his foes. With revilement and torture let us put the just one to the test that we may have proof of his gentleness and try his patience. Let us condemn him to a shameful death; for according to his own words, God will take care of him.

Responsorial Psalm: Psalm 54:3-4, 5, 6 and 8

R. (6b) The Lord upholds my life.

O God, by your name save me, and by your might defend my cause. O God, hear my prayer; hearken to the words of my mouth. **R.**

For the haughty men have risen up against me, the ruthless seek my life; they set not God before their eyes. **R.**

Behold, God is my helper; the Lord sustains my life. Freely will I offer you sacrifice; I will praise your name, O LORD, for its goodness. **R.**

Second Reading: James 3:16-4:3

Beloved: Where jealousy and selfish ambition exist, there is disorder and every foul practice. But the wisdom from above is first of all pure, then peaceable, gentle, compliant, full of mercy and good fruits, without inconstancy or insincerity. And the fruit of righteousness is sown in peace for those who cultivate peace. Where do the wars and where do the conflicts among you come from? Is it not from your passions that make war within your members? You covet but do not possess. You kill and envy but you cannot obtain; you fight and wage war. You do not possess because you do not ask. You ask but do not receive, because you ask wrongly, to spend it on your passions.

Alleluia: 2 Thessalonians 2:14

R. Alleluia, alleluia.

God has called us through the Gospel to possess the glory of our Lord Jesus Christ. **R.**

Gospel: Mark 9:30-37

Jesus and his disciples left from there and began a journey through Galilee, but he did not wish anyone to know about it. He was teaching his disciples and telling them, "The Son of Man is to be handed over to men and they will kill him, and three days after his death the Son of Man will rise." But they did not understand the saying, and they were afraid to question him. They came to Capernaum and, once inside the house, he began to ask them, "What were you arguing about on the way?" But they remained silent. They had been discussing among themselves on the way who was the greatest. Then he sat down, called the Twelve, and said to them, "If anyone wishes to be first, he shall be the last of all and the servant of all." Taking a child, he placed it in the their midst, and putting his arms around it, he said to them, "Whoever receives one child such as this in my name, receives me; and whoever receives me, receives not me but the One who sent me."

TUESDAY, SEPTEMBER 21

FEAST OF SAINT MATTHEW, APOSTLE AND EVANGELIST

First Reading: Ephesians 4:1-7, 11-13

Brothers and sisters: I, a prisoner for the Lord, urge you to live in a manner worthy of the call you have received, with all humility and gentleness, with patience, bearing with one another through love, striving to preserve the unity of the Spirit through the bond of peace: one Body and one Spirit, as you were also called to the one hope of your call; one Lord, one faith, one baptism; one God and Father of all, who is over all and through all and in all. But grace was given to each of us according to the measure of Christ's gift. And he gave some as Apostles, others as prophets, others as evangelists, others as pastors and teachers, to equip the holy ones for the work of ministry, for building up the Body of Christ, until we all attain to the unity of faith and knowledge of the Son of God, to mature manhood, to the extent of the full stature of Christ.

Responsorial Psalm: Psalm 19:2-3, 4-5

R. (5) Their message goes out through all the earth.

The heavens declare the glory of God; and the firmament proclaims his handiwork. Day pours out the word to day, and night to night imparts knowledge. **R.**

Not a word nor a discourse whose voice is not heard;

through all the earth their voice resounds, and to the ends of the world, their message. **R.**

Alleluia

R. Alleluia, alleluia.

We praise you, O God, we acclaim you as Lord; the glorious company of Apostles praise you. **R.**

Gospel: Matthew 9:9-13

As Jesus passed by, he saw a man named Matthew sitting at the customs post. He said to him, "Follow me." And he got up and followed him. While he was at table in his house, many tax collectors and sinners came and sat with Jesus and his disciples. The Pharisees saw this and said to his disciples, "Why does your teacher eat with tax collectors and sinners?" He heard this and said, "Those who are well do not need a physician, but the sick do. Go and learn the meaning of the words, *I desire mercy, not sacrifice.* I did not come to call the righteous but sinners."

TWENTY-SIXTH SUNDAY IN ORDINARY TIME

First Reading: Numbers 11:25-29

The LORD came down in the cloud and spoke to Moses. Taking some of the spirit that was on Moses, the LORD bestowed it on the seventy elders; and as the spirit came to rest on them, they prophesied. Now two men, one named Eldad and the other Medad, were not in the gathering but had been left in the camp. They too had been on the list, but had not gone out to the tent; yet the spirit came to rest on them also, and they prophesied in the camp. So, when a young man quickly told Moses, "Eldad and Medad are prophesying in the camp," Joshua, son of Nun, who from his youth had been Moses' aide, said, "Moses, my lord, stop them." But Moses answered him, "Are you jealous for my sake? Would that all the people of the LORD were prophets! Would that the LORD might bestow his spirit on them all!"

Responsorial Psalm: Psalm 19:8, 10, 12-13, 14

R. (9a) The precepts of the Lord give joy to the heart.

The law of the LORD is perfect, refreshing the soul; the decree of the LORD is trustworthy, giving wisdom to the simple. **R.**

The fear of the LORD is pure, enduring forever; the

ordinances of the LORD are true, all of them just. **R.**

Though your servant is careful of them, very diligent in keeping them, yet who can detect failings? Cleanse me from my unknown faults! **R.**

From wanton sin especially, restrain your servant; let it not rule over me. Then shall I be blameless and innocent of serious sin. **R.**

Second Reading: James 5:1-6

Come now, you rich, weep and wail over your impending miseries. Your wealth has rotted away, your clothes have become moth-eaten, your gold and silver have corroded, and that corrosion will be a testimony against you; it will devour your flesh like a fire. You have stored up treasure for the last days. Behold, the wages you withheld from the workers who harvested your fields are crying aloud; and the cries of the harvesters have reached the ears of the Lord of hosts. You have lived on earth in luxury and pleasure; you have fattened your hearts for the day of slaughter. You have condemned; you have murdered the righteous one; he offers you no resistance.

Alleluia: John 17:17b, 17a
R. Alleluia, alleluia.

Your word, O Lord, is truth; consecrate us in the truth. **R.**

Gospel: Mark 9:38-43, 45, 47-48

At that time, John said to Jesus, "Teacher, we saw someone driving out demons in your name, and we tried to prevent him because he does not follow us." Jesus replied, "Do not prevent him. There is no one who performs a mighty deed in my name who can at the same time speak ill of me. For whoever is not against us is for us. Anyone who gives you a cup of water to drink because you belong to Christ, amen, I say to you, will surely not lose his reward. "Whoever causes one of these little ones who believe in me to sin, it would be better for him if a great millstone were put around his neck and he were thrown into the sea. If your hand causes you to sin, cut it off. It is better for you to enter into life maimed than with two hands to go into Gehenna, into the unquenchable fire. And if your foot causes you to sin, cut if off. It is better for you to enter into life crippled than with two feet to be thrown into Gehenna. And if your eye causes you to sin, pluck it out. Better for you to enter into the kingdom of God with one eye than with two eyes to be thrown into Gehenna, where 'their worm does not die, and the fire is not quenched.'"

WEDNESDAY, SEPTEMBER 29

FEAST OF SAINTS MICHAEL, GABRIEL, AND RAPHAEL, ARCHANGELS

First Reading: Daniel 7:9-10, 13-14 or Revelation 12:7-12ab

As I watched: Thrones were set up and the Ancient One took his throne. His clothing was bright as snow, and the hair on his head as white as wool; His throne was flames of fire, with wheels of burning fire. A surging stream of fire flowed out from where he sat; Thousands upon thousands were ministering to him, and myriads upon myriads attended him. The court was convened, and the books were opened. As the visions during the night continued, I saw one like a son of man coming, on the clouds of heaven; when he reached the Ancient One and was presented before him, He received dominion, glory, and kingship; nations and peoples of every language serve him. His dominion is an everlasting dominion that shall not be taken away, his kingship shall not be destroyed.

Or:

Revelation 12:7-12ab

War broke out in heaven; Michael and his angels battled against the dragon. The dragon and its angels fought back, but they did not prevail and there was no longer any place for them in heaven. The huge dragon, the ancient serpent, who is called the Devil and Satan, who deceived the whole world, was thrown down to earth, and its angels were thrown down with it. Then I heard a loud voice in heaven say: "Now have salvation and power come, and the Kingdom of our God and the authority of his Anointed. For the accuser of our brothers is cast out, who accuses them before our God day and night. They conquered him by the Blood of the Lamb and by the word of their testimony; love for life did not deter them from death. Therefore, rejoice, you heavens, and you who dwell in them."

Responsorial Psalm: Psalm 138:1-2ab, 2cde-3, 4-5

R. (1) In the sight of the angels I will sing your praises, Lord.

I will give thanks to you, O LORD, with all my heart, for you have heard the words of my mouth; in the presence of the angels I will sing your praise; I will worship at your holy temple and give thanks to your name. **R.**

Because of your kindness and your truth; for you have made great above all things your name and your promise. When I called, you answered me; you built up strength within me. **R.**

All the kings of the earth shall give thanks to you, O LORD when they hear the words of your mouth; and they shall sing of the ways of the LORD "Great is the glory of the LORD **R.**

Alleluia: Psalm 103:21
R. Alleluia, alleluia.

Bless the LORD, all you angels, you ministers, who do his will. **R.**

Gospel: John 1:47-51

Jesus saw Nathanael coming toward him and said of him, "Here is a true child of Israel. There is no duplicity in him." Nathanael said to him, "How do you know me?" Jesus answered and said to him, "Before Philip called you, I saw you under the fig tree." Nathanael answered him, "Rabbi, you are the Son of God; you are the King of Israel." Jesus answered and said to him, "Do you believe because I told you that I saw you under the fig tree? You will see greater things than this." And he said to him, "Amen, amen, I say to you, you will see heaven opened and the angels of God ascending and descending on the Son of Man."

OCTOBER

TWENTY-SEVENTH SUNDAY IN ORDINARY TIME

First Reading: Genesis 2:18-24

The LORD God said: "It is not good for the man to be alone. I will make a suitable partner for him." So, the LORD God formed out of the ground various wild animals and various birds of the air, and he brought them to the man to see what he would call them; whatever the man called each of them would be its name. The man gave names to all the cattle, all the birds of the air, and all wild animals; but none proved to be the suitable partner for the man. So, the LORD God cast a deep sleep on the man, and while he was asleep, he took out one of his ribs and closed up its place with flesh. The LORD God then built up into a woman the rib that he had taken from the man. When he brought her to the man, the man said: "This one, at last, is bone of my bones and flesh of my flesh; this one shall be called 'woman,' for out of 'her man' this one has been taken." That is why a man leaves his father and mother and clings to his wife, and the two of them become one flesh.

Responsorial Psalm: Psalm 128:1-2, 3, 4-5, 6

R. (5) May the Lord bless us all the days of our lives.

Blessed are you who fear the LORD, who walk in his ways!
For you shall eat the fruit of your handiwork; blessed shall
you be, and favored. **R.**

Your wife shall be like a fruitful vine in the recesses of your
home; your children like olive plants around your table. **R.**

Behold, thus is the man blessed who fears the LORD. The
LORD bless you from Zion: may you see the prosperity of
Jerusalem all the days of your life. **R.**

May you see your children's children. Peace be upon Israel!
R.

Second Reading: Hebrews 2:9-11

Brothers and sisters: He "for a little while" was made "lower
than the angels," that by the grace of God he might taste
death for everyone. For it was fitting that he, for whom and
through whom all things exist, in bringing many children to
glory, should make the leader to their salvation perfect
through suffering. He who consecrates and those who are
being consecrated all have one origin. Therefore, he is not
ashamed to call them "brothers."

Alleluia: 1 John 4:12
R. Alleluia, alleluia.

If we love one another, God remains in us and his love is brought to perfection in us. **R.**

Gospel: Mark 10:2-16 or 10:2-12

The Pharisees approached Jesus and asked, "Is it lawful for a husband to divorce his wife?" They were testing him. He said to them in reply, "What did Moses command you?" They replied, "Moses permitted a husband to write a bill of divorce and dismiss her." But Jesus told them, "Because of the hardness of your hearts he wrote you this commandment. But from the beginning of creation, God made them male and female. *For this reason, a man shall leave his father and mother and be joined to his wife, and the two shall become one flesh.* So, they are no longer two but one flesh. Therefore, what God has joined together, no human being must separate." In the house the disciples again questioned Jesus about this. He said to them, "Whoever divorces his wife and marries another commits adultery against her; and if she divorces her husband and marries another, she commits adultery." And people were bringing children to him that he might touch them, but the disciples rebuked them. When Jesus saw this, he became indignant and said to them, "Let the children come to me; do not prevent them, for the kingdom of God belongs to such as these. Amen, I say to you, whoever does not accept the kingdom of God like a child will not enter it." Then he embraced them and blessed them, placing his hands on them.

Or:

Mark 10:2-12

The Pharisees approached Jesus and asked, "Is it lawful for a husband to divorce his wife?" They were testing him. He said to them in reply, "What did Moses command you?" They replied, "Moses permitted a husband to write a bill of divorce and dismiss her." But Jesus told them, "Because of the hardness of your hearts he wrote you this commandment. But from the beginning of creation, God made them male and female. *For this reason, a man shall leave his father and mother and be joined to his wife, and the two shall become one flesh.* So, they are no longer two but one flesh. Therefore, what God has joined together, no human being must separate." In the house the disciples again questioned Jesus about this. He said to them, "Whoever divorces his wife and marries another commits adultery against her; and if she divorces her husband and marries another, she commits adultery."

TWENTY-EIGHTH SUNDAY IN ORDINARY TIME

First Reading: Wisdom 7:7-11

I prayed, and prudence was given me; I pleaded, and the spirit of wisdom came to me. I preferred her to scepter and throne, and deemed riches nothing in comparison with her, nor did I liken any priceless gem to her; because all gold, in view of her, is a little sand, and before her, silver is to be accounted mire. Beyond health and comeliness I loved her, and I chose to have her rather than the light, because the splendor of her never yields to sleep. Yet all good things together came to me in her company, and countless riches at her hands.

Responsorial Psalm: Psalm 90:12-13, 14-15, 16-17

R. (14) Fill us with your love, O Lord, and we will sing for joy!

Teach us to number our days aright, that we may gain wisdom of heart. Return, O LORD! How long? Have pity on your servants! **R.**

Fill us at daybreak with your kindness, that we may shout for joy and gladness all our days. Make us glad, for the days when you afflicted us, for the years when we saw evil. **R.**

Let your work be seen by your servants and your glory by their children; and may the gracious care of the LORD our God be ours; prosper the work of our hands for us! Prosper the work of our hands! **R.**

Second Reading: Hebrews 4:12-13

Brothers and sisters: Indeed, the word of God is living and effective, sharper than any two-edged sword, penetrating even between soul and spirit, joints and marrow, and able to discern reflections and thoughts of the heart. No creature is concealed from him, but everything is naked and exposed to the eyes of him to whom we must render an account.

Alleluia: Matthew 5:3

R. Alleluia, alleluia.

Blessed are the poor in spirit, for theirs is the kingdom of heaven. **R.**

Gospel: Mark 10:17-30 or 10:17-27

As Jesus was setting out on a journey, a man ran up, knelt down before him, and asked him, "Good teacher, what must I do to inherit eternal life?" Jesus answered him, "Why do you call me good? No one is good but God alone. You know the commandments: *You shall not kill; you shall not commit adultery; you shall not steal; you shall not bear false witness; you shall not defraud; honor your father and your mother."* He replied and said to him, "Teacher, all of these I have observed from my youth." Jesus, looking at him, loved him and said to him, "You are lacking in one thing. Go, sell what you have, and give to the poor and you will have treasure in heaven; then come, follow me." At that statement his face fell, and he went away sad, for he had many possessions. Jesus looked around and said to his disciples, "How hard it is for those who have wealth to enter the kingdom of God!" The disciples were amazed at his words. So, Jesus again said to them in reply, "Children, how hard it is to enter the kingdom of God! It is easier for a camel to pass through the eye of a needle than for one who is rich to enter the kingdom of God." They were exceedingly astonished and said among themselves, "Then who can be saved?" Jesus looked at them and said, "For human beings it is impossible, but not for God. All things are possible for God." Peter began to say to him, "We have given up everything and followed you." Jesus said, "Amen, I say to you, there is no one who has given up house or brothers or sisters or mother or father or children or lands for my sake and for the sake of the gospel who will not receive a hundred times more now in this present age: houses and brothers and sisters and mothers and children and lands, with persecutions, and eternal life in the age to come."

Or:

Mark 10:17-27

As Jesus was setting out on a journey, a man ran up, knelt down before him, and asked him, "Good teacher, what must I do to inherit eternal life?" Jesus answered him, "Why do you call me good? No one is good but God alone. You know the commandments: *You shall not kill; you shall not commit adultery; you shall not steal; you shall not bear false witness; you shall not defraud; honor your father and your mother.*" He replied and said to him, "Teacher, all of these I have observed from my youth." Jesus, looking at him, loved him and said to him, "You are lacking in one thing. Go, sell what you have, and give to the poor and you will have treasure in heaven; then come, follow me." At that statement his face fell, and he went away sad, for he had many possessions. Jesus looked around and said to his disciples, "How hard it is for those who have wealth to enter the kingdom of God!" The disciples were amazed at his words. So, Jesus again said to them in reply, "Children, how hard it is to enter the kingdom of God! It is easier for a camel to pass through the eye of a needle than for one who is rich to enter the kingdom of God." They were exceedingly astonished and said among themselves, "Then who can be saved?" Jesus looked at them and said, "For human beings it is impossible, but not for God. All things are possible for God."

SUNDAY, OCTOBER 17
TWENTY-NINTH SUNDAY IN ORDINARY TIME
First Reading: Isaiah Is 53:10-11

The LORD was pleased to crush him in infirmity. If he gives his life as an offering for sin, he shall see his descendants in a long life, and the will of the LORD shall be accomplished through him. Because of his affliction he shall see the light in fullness of days; through his suffering, my servant shall justify many, and their guilt he shall bear.

Responsorial Psalm: Psalm 33:4-5, 18-19, 20, 22
R. (22) Lord, let your mercy be on us, as we place our trust in you.

Upright is the word of the LORD, and all his works are trustworthy. He loves justice and right; of the kindness of the LORD the earth is full. **R.**

See, the eyes of the LORD are upon those who fear him, upon those who hope for his kindness, to deliver them from death and preserve them in spite of famine. **R.**

Our soul waits for the LORD, who is our help and our shield. May your kindness, O LORD, be upon us who have put our hope in you. **R.**

Second Reading: Hebrews 4:14-16

Brothers and sisters: Since we have a great high priest who has passed through the heavens, Jesus, the Son of God, let us hold fast to our confession. For we do not have a high priest who is unable to sympathize with our weaknesses, but one who has similarly been tested in every way, yet without sin. So, let us confidently approach the throne of grace to receive mercy and to find grace for timely help.

Alleluia: Mark 10:45
R. Alleluia, alleluia.

The Son of Man came to serve and to give his life as a ransom for many. **R.**

Gospel: Mark 10:35-45 or 10:42-45

James and John, the sons of Zebedee, came to Jesus and said to him, "Teacher, we want you to do for us whatever we ask of you." He replied, "What do you wish me to do for you?" They answered him, "Grant that in your glory we may sit one at your right and the other at your left." Jesus said to them, "You do not know what you are asking. Can you drink the cup that I drink or be baptized with the baptism with which I am baptized?" They said to him, "We can." Jesus said to them, "The cup that I drink, you will drink, and with the baptism with which I am baptized, you will be baptized; but to sit at my right or at my left is not mine to give but is for those for whom it has been prepared." When the ten heard this, they became indignant at James and John. Jesus summoned them and said to them, "You know that those who are recognized as rulers over the Gentiles lord it over them, and their great ones make their authority over them felt. But it shall not be so among you. Rather, whoever wishes to be great among you will be your servant; whoever wishes to be first among you will be the slave of all. For the Son of Man did not come to be served but to serve and to give his life as a ransom for many."

Or:
Mark 10:42-45

Jesus summoned the twelve and said to them, "You know that those who are recognized as rulers over the Gentiles lord it over them, and their great ones make their authority over them felt. But it shall not be so among you. Rather, whoever wishes to be great among you will be your servant;

whoever wishes to be first among you will be the slave of all. For the Son of Man did not come to be served but to serve and to give his life as a ransom for many."

MONDAY, OCTOBER 18
FEAST OF SAINT LUKE, EVANGELIST

First Reading: 2 Timothy 4:10-17b

Beloved: Demas, enamored of the present world, deserted me and went to Thessalonica, Crescens to Galatia, and Titus to Dalmatia. Luke is the only one with me. Get Mark and bring him with you, for he is helpful to me in the ministry. I have sent Tychicus to Ephesus. When you come, bring the cloak I left with Carpus in Troas, the papyrus rolls, and especially the parchments. Alexander the coppersmith did me a great deal of harm; the Lord will repay him according to his deeds. You too be on guard against him, for he has strongly resisted our preaching. At my first defense no one appeared on my behalf, but everyone deserted me. May it not be held against them! But the Lord stood by me and gave me strength, so that through me the proclamation might be completed and all the Gentiles might hear it.

Responsorial Psalm: Psalm 145:10-11, 12-13, 17-18

R. (12) Your friends make known, O Lord, the glorious splendor of your Kingdom.

Let all your works give you thanks, O LORD, and let your faithful ones bless you. Let them discourse of the glory of your Kingdom and speak of your might. **R.**

Making known to men your might and the glorious splendor of your Kingdom. Your Kingdom is a Kingdom for all ages, and your dominion endures through all generations. **R.**

The LORD is just in all his ways and holy in all his works. The LORD is near to all who call upon him, to all who call upon him in truth. **R.**

Alleluia: John 15:16
R. Alleluia, alleluia.

I chose you from the world, to go and bear fruit that will last, says the Lord. **R.**

Gospel: Luke 10:1-9

The Lord Jesus appointed seventy-two disciples whom he sent ahead of him in pairs to every town and place he intended to visit. He said to them, "The harvest is abundant but the laborers are few; so, ask the master of the harvest to send out laborers for his harvest. Go on your way; behold, I am sending you like lambs among wolves. Carry no money bag, no sack, no sandals; and greet no one along the way. Into whatever house you enter, first say, 'Peace to this household.' If a peaceful person lives there, your peace will rest on him; but if not, it will return to you. Stay in the same house and eat and drink what is offered to you, for the laborer deserves payment. Do not move about from one house to another. Whatever town you enter and they welcome you, eat what is set before you, cure the sick in it and say to them, 'The Kingdom of God is at hand for you.'"

SUNDAY, OCTOBER 24
THIRTIETH SUNDAY IN ORDINARY TIME
First Reading: Jeremiah 31:7-9

Thus says the LORD: Shout with joy for Jacob, exult at the head of the nations; proclaim your praise and say: The LORD has delivered his people, the remnant of Israel. Behold, I will bring them back from the land of the north; I will gather them from the ends of the world, with the blind and the lame in their midst, the mothers and those with child; they shall return as an immense throng. They departed in tears, but I will console them and guide them; I will lead them to brooks of water, on a level road, so that none shall stumble. For I am a father to Israel, Ephraim is my first-born.

Responsorial Psalm: Psalm 126:1-2, 2-3, 4-5, 6

R. (3) The Lord has done great things for us; we are filled with joy.

When the LORD brought back the captives of Zion, we were like men dreaming. Then our mouth was filled with laughter, and our tongue with rejoicing. **R.**

Then they said among the nations, "The LORD has done great things for them." The LORD has done great things for us; we are glad indeed. **R.**

Restore our fortunes, O LORD, like the torrents in the southern desert. Those that sow in tears shall reap rejoicing. **R.**

Although they go forth weeping, carrying the seed to be sown, they shall come back rejoicing, carrying their sheaves. **R.**

Second Reading: Hebrews 5:1-6

Brothers and sisters: Every high priest is taken from among men and made their representative before God, to offer gifts and sacrifices for sins. He is able to deal patiently with the ignorant and erring, for he himself is beset by weakness and so, for this reason, must make sin offerings for himself as well as for the people. No one takes this honor upon himself but only when called by God, just as Aaron was. In the same way, it was not Christ who glorified himself in becoming high priest, but rather the one who said to him: *You are my son: this day I have begotten you;* just as he says in another place: *You are a priest forever according to the order of Melchizedek.*

Alleluia: 2 Timothy 1:10
R. Alleluia, alleluia.
Our Savior Jesus Christ destroyed death and brought life to light through the Gospel. **R.**

Gospel: Mark 10:46-52
As Jesus was leaving Jericho with his disciples and a sizable crowd, Bartimaeus, a blind man, the son of Timaeus, sat by the roadside begging. On hearing that it was Jesus of Nazareth, he began to cry out and say, "Jesus, son of David, have pity on me." And many rebuked him, telling him to be silent. But he kept calling out all the more, "Son of David, have pity on me." Jesus stopped and said, "Call him." So they called the blind man, saying to him, "Take courage; get up, Jesus is calling you." He threw aside his cloak, sprang up, and came to Jesus. Jesus said to him in reply, "What do you want me to do for you?" The blind man replied to him, "Master, I want to see." Jesus told him, "Go your way; your

faith has saved you." Immediately he received his sight and followed him on the way.

THURSDAY, OCTOBER 28
FEAST OF SAINTS SIMON AND JUDE, APOSTLES
First Reading: Ephesians 2:19-22

Brothers and sisters: You are no longer strangers and sojourners, but you are fellow citizens with the holy ones and members of the household of God, built upon the foundation of the Apostles and prophets, with Christ Jesus himself as the capstone. Through him the whole structure is held together and grows into a temple sacred in the Lord; in him you also are being built together into a dwelling place of God in the Spirit.

Responsorial Psalm: Psalm 19:2-3, 4-5
R. (5a) Their message goes out through all the earth.
The heavens declare the glory of God, and the firmament proclaims his handiwork. Day pours out the word to day, and night to night imparts knowledge. **R.**
Not a word nor a discourse whose voice is not heard; through all the earth their voice resounds, and to the ends of the world, their message. **R.**

Alleluia

R. Alleluia, alleluia.

We praise you, O God, we acclaim you as Lord; the glorious company of Apostles praise you. **R.**

Gospel: Luke 6:12-16

Jesus went up to the mountain to pray, and he spent the night in prayer to God. When day came, he called his disciples to himself, and from them he chose Twelve, whom he also named Apostles: Simon, whom he named Peter, and his brother Andrew, James, John, Philip, Bartholomew, Matthew, Thomas, James the son of Alphaeus, Simon who was called a Zealot, and Judas the son of James, and Judas Iscariot, who became a traitor.

SUNDAY, OCTOBER 31

THIRTY-FIRST SUNDAY IN ORDINARY TIME

First Reading: Deuteronomy 6:2-6

Moses spoke to the people, saying: "Fear the LORD, your God, and keep, throughout the days of your lives, all his statutes and commandments which I enjoin on you, and thus have long life. Hear then, Israel, and be careful to observe them, that you may grow and prosper the more, in keeping with the promise of the LORD, the God of your fathers, to give you a land flowing with milk and honey. "Hear, O Israel! The LORD is our God, the LORD alone! Therefore, you shall love the LORD, your God, with all your heart, and with all your soul, and with all your strength. Take to heart these words which I enjoin on you today."

Responsorial Psalm: Psalm 18:2-3, 3-4, 47, 51

R. (2) I love you, Lord, my strength.

I love you, O LORD, my strength, O LORD, my rock, my fortress, my deliverer. **R.**

My God, my rock of refuge, my shield, the horn of my salvation, my stronghold! Praised be the LORD, I exclaim, and I am safe from my enemies. **R.**

The LORD lives! And blessed be my rock! Extolled be God my savior. You who gave great victories to your king and showed kindness to your anointed. **R.**

Second Reading: Hebrews 7:23-28

Brothers and sisters: The Levitical priests were many because they were prevented by death from remaining in office, but Jesus, because he remains forever, has a priesthood that does not pass away. Therefore, he is always able to save those who approach God through him, since he lives forever to make intercession for them. It was fitting that we should have such a high priest: holy, innocent, undefiled, separated from sinners, higher than the heavens. He has no need, as did the high priests, to offer sacrifice day after day, first for his own sins and then for those of the people; he did that once for all when he offered himself. For the law appoints men subject to weakness to be high priests, but the word of the oath, which was taken after the law, appoints a son, who has been made perfect forever.

Alleluia: John 14:23

R. Alleluia, alleluia.

Whoever loves me will keep my word, says the Lord; and my father will love him and we will come to him. **R.**

Gospel: Mark 12:28b-34

One of the scribes came to Jesus and asked him, "Which is the first of all the commandments?" Jesus replied, "The first is this: *Hear, O Israel! The Lord our God is Lord alone! You shall love the Lord your God with all your heart, with all your soul, with all your mind, and with all your strength.* The second is this: *You shall love your neighbor as yourself.* There is no other commandment greater than these." The scribe said to him, "Well said, teacher. You are right in saying, 'He is One and there is no other than he.' And 'to love him with all your heart, with all your understanding, with all your strength, and to love your neighbor as yourself' is worth more than all burnt offerings and sacrifices." And when Jesus saw that he answered with understanding, he said to him, "You are not far from the kingdom of God." And no one dared to ask him any more questions.

NOVEMBER

MONDAY, NOVEMBER 1

SOLEMNITY OF ALL SAINTS

First Reading: Revelation 7:2-4, 9-14

I, John, saw another angel come up from the East, holding the seal of the living God. He cried out in a loud voice to the four angels who were given power to damage the land and the sea, "Do not damage the land or the sea or the trees until we put the seal on the foreheads of the servants of our God." I heard the number of those who had been marked with the seal, one hundred and forty-four thousand marked from every tribe of the children of Israel. After this I had a vision of a great multitude, which no one could count, from every nation, race, people, and tongue. They stood before the throne and before the Lamb, wearing white robes and holding palm branches in their hands. They cried out in a loud voice: "Salvation comes from our God, who is seated on the throne, and from the Lamb." All the angels stood around the throne and around the elders and the four living creatures. They prostrated themselves before the throne, worshiped God, and exclaimed: "Amen. Blessing and glory, wisdom and thanksgiving, honor, power, and might be to our God forever and ever. Amen." Then one of the elders spoke up and said to me, "Who are these wearing white robes, and where did they come from?" I said to him, "My lord, you are the one who knows." He said to me, "These are the ones who have survived the time of great distress; they have washed their robes and made them white in the Blood of the Lamb."

Responsorial Psalm: Psalm 24:1bc-2, 3-4ab, 5-6
R. (6) Lord, this is the people that longs to see your face.
The LORD's are the earth and its fullness; the world and those who dwell in it. For he founded it upon the seas and established it upon the rivers. **R.**
Who can ascend the mountain of the LORD? Or who may stand in his holy place? One whose hands are sinless, whose heart is clean, who desires not what is vain. **R.**
He shall receive a blessing from the LORD, a reward from God his savior. Such is the race that seeks him, that seeks the face of the God of Jacob. **R.**

Second Reading: 1 John 3:1-3
Beloved: See what love the Father has bestowed on us that we may be called the children of God. Yet so we are. The reason the world does not know us is that it did not know him. Beloved, we are God's children now; what we shall be has not yet been revealed. We do know that when it is

revealed we shall be like him, for we shall see him as he is. Everyone who has this hope based on him makes himself pure, as he is pure.

Alleluia: Matthew 11:28
R. Alleluia, alleluia.
Come to me, all you who labor and are burdened, and I will give you rest, says the Lord. **R.**

Gospel: Matthew 5:1-12a
When Jesus saw the crowds, he went up the mountain, and after he had sat down, his disciples came to him. He began to teach them, saying: "Blessed are the poor in spirit, for theirs is the Kingdom of heaven.

Blessed are they who mourn, for they will be comforted.

Blessed are the meek, for they will inherit the land.

Blessed are they who hunger and thirst for righteousness, for they will be satisfied. Blessed are the merciful, for they will be shown mercy.

Blessed are the clean of heart, for they will see God.

Blessed are the peacemakers, for they will be called children of God.

Blessed are they who are persecuted for the sake of righteousness, for theirs is the Kingdom of heaven. Blessed are you when they insult you and persecute you and utter every kind of evil against you falsely because of me. Rejoice and be glad, for your reward will be great in heaven."

TUESDAY, NOVEMBER 2
THE COMMEMORATION OF ALL THE FAITHFUL DEPARTED (All Souls)
First Reading: Wisdom 3:1-9

The souls of the just are in the hand of God, and no torment shall touch them. They seemed, in the view of the foolish, to be dead; and their passing away was thought an affliction and their going forth from us, utter destruction. But they are in peace. For if before men, indeed, they be punished, yet is their hope full of immortality; chastised a little, they shall be greatly blessed, because God tried them and found them worthy of himself. As gold in the furnace, he proved them, and as sacrificial offerings he took them to himself. In the time of their visitation they shall shine, and shall dart about as sparks through stubble; they shall judge nations and rule over peoples, and the LORD shall be their King forever. Those who trust in him shall understand truth, and the faithful shall abide with him in love: because grace and mercy are with his holy ones, and his care is with his elect.

Responsorial Psalm: Psalm 23:1-3a, 3b-4, 5, 6

R. (1) The Lord is my shepherd; there is nothing I shall want.

Or:

R. Though I walk in the valley of darkness, I fear no evil, for you are with me.

The LORD is my shepherd; I shall not want. In verdant pastures he gives me repose; beside restful waters he leads me; he refreshes my soul. **R.**

He guides me in right paths for his name's sake. Even though I walk in the dark valley I fear no evil; for you are at my side with your rod and your staff that give me courage. **R.**

You spread the table before me in the sight of my foes; you anoint my head with oil; my cup overflows. **R.**

Only goodness and kindness follow me all the days of my life; and I shall dwell in the house of the LORD for years to come. **R.**

Second Reading: Romans 5:5-11

Brothers and sisters: Hope does not disappoint, because the love of God has been poured out into our hearts through the Holy Spirit that has been given to us. For Christ, while we were still helpless, died at the appointed time for the ungodly. Indeed, only with difficulty does one die for a just person, though perhaps for a good person one might even find courage to die. But God proves his love for us in that while we were still sinners Christ died for us. How much more then, since we are now justified by his Blood, will we be saved through him from the wrath. Indeed, if, while we were enemies, we were reconciled to God through the death of his Son, how much more, once reconciled, will we be saved by his life. Not only that, but we also boast of God through our Lord Jesus Christ, through whom we have now received reconciliation.

Alleluia: Matthew 25:34
R. Alleluia, alleluia.
Come, you who are blessed by my Father; inherit the Kingdom prepared for you from the foundation of the world. **R.**

Gospel: John 6:37-40
Jesus said to the crowds: "Everything that the Father gives me will come to me, and I will not reject anyone who comes to me, because I came down from heaven not to do my own will but the will of the one who sent me. And this is the will of the one who sent me, that I should not lose anything of

what he gave me, but that I should raise it on the last day. For this is the will of my Father, that everyone who sees the Son and believes in him may have eternal life, and I shall raise him on the last day."

SUNDAY, NOVEMBER 7
THIRTY-SECOND SUNDAY IN ORDINARY TIME
First Reading: 1 Kings 17:10-16

In those days, Elijah the prophet went to Zarephath. As he arrived at the entrance of the city, a widow was gathering sticks there; he called out to her, "Please bring me a small cupful of water to drink." She left to get it, and he called out after her, "Please bring along a bit of bread." She answered, "As the LORD, your God, lives, I have nothing baked; there is only a handful of flour in my jar and a little oil in my jug. Just now I was collecting a couple of sticks, to go in and prepare something for myself and my son; when we have eaten it, we shall die." Elijah said to her, "Do not be afraid. Go and do as you propose. But first make me a little cake and bring it to me. Then you can prepare something for yourself and your son. For the LORD, the God of Israel, says, 'The jar of flour shall not go empty, nor the jug of oil run dry, until the day when the LORD sends rain upon the earth.'" She left and did as Elijah had said. She was able to eat for a year, and he and her son as well; the jar of flour did not go empty, nor the jug of oil run dry, as the LORD had foretold through Elijah.

Responsorial Psalm: Psalm 146:7, 8-9, 9-10

R. (1b) Praise the Lord, my soul!

Or:

R. Alleluia.

The LORD keeps faith forever, secures justice for the oppressed, gives food to the hungry. The LORD sets captives free. **R.**

The LORD gives sight to the blind. The LORD raises up those who were bowed down; the LORD loves the just. The LORD protects strangers. **R.**

The fatherless and the widow he sustains, but the way of the wicked he thwarts. The LORD shall reign forever; your God, O Zion, through all generations. Alleluia. **R.**

Second Reading: Hebrews 9:24-28

Christ did not enter into a sanctuary made by hands, a copy of the true one, but heaven itself, that he might now appear before God on our behalf. Not that he might offer himself repeatedly, as the high priest enters each year into the sanctuary with blood that is not his own; if that were so, he would have had to suffer repeatedly from the foundation of the world. But now once for all he has appeared at the end of the ages to take away sin by his sacrifice. Just as it is appointed that human beings die once, and after this the judgment, so also Christ, offered once to take away the sins of many, will appear a second time, not to take away sin but to bring salvation to those who eagerly await him.

Alleluia: Matthew 5:3
R. Alleluia, alleluia.
Blessed are the poor in spirit, for theirs is the kingdom of heaven. **R.**

Gospel: Mark 12:38-44 or 12:41-44
In the course of his teaching Jesus said to the crowds, "Beware of the scribes, who like to go around in long robes and accept greetings in the marketplaces, seats of honor in synagogues, and places of honor at banquets. They devour the houses of widows and, as a pretext recite lengthy prayers. They will receive a very severe condemnation." He sat down opposite the treasury and observed how the crowd put money into the treasury. Many rich people put in large sums. A poor widow also came and put in two small coins worth a few cents. Calling his disciples to himself, he said to

them, "Amen, I say to you, this poor widow put in more than all the other contributors to the treasury. For they have all contributed from their surplus wealth, but she, from her poverty, has contributed all she had, her whole livelihood."

Or:
Mark 12:41-44

Jesus sat down opposite the treasury and observed how the crowd put money into the treasury. Many rich people put in large sums. A poor widow also came and put in two small coins worth a few cents. Calling his disciples to himself, he said to them, "Amen, I say to you, this poor widow put in more than all the other contributors to the treasury. For they have all contributed from their surplus wealth, but she, from her poverty, has contributed all she had, her whole livelihood."

TUESDAY, NOVEMBER 9
FEAST OF THE DEDICATION OF THE LATERAN BASILICA IN ROME
First Reading: Ezekiel 47:1-2, 8-9, 12

The angel brought me back to the entrance of the temple, and I saw water flowing out from beneath the threshold of the temple toward the east, for the façade of the temple was toward the east; the water flowed down from the southern side of the temple, south of the altar. He led me outside by the north gate, and around to the outer gate facing the east, where I saw water trickling from the southern side. He said to me, "This water flows into the eastern district down upon the Arabah, and empties into the sea, the salt waters, which it makes fresh. Wherever the river flows, every sort of living creature that can multiply shall live, and there shall be abundant fish, for wherever this water comes the sea shall be made fresh. Along both banks of the river, fruit trees of every kind shall grow; their leaves shall not fade, nor their fruit fail. Every month they shall bear fresh fruit, for they shall be watered by the flow from the sanctuary. Their fruit shall serve for food, and their leaves for medicine."

Responsorial Psalm: Psalm 46:2-3, 5-6, 8-9
R. (5) The waters of the river gladden the city of God, the holy dwelling of the Most High!
God is our refuge and our strength, an ever-present help in distress. Therefore, we fear not, though the earth be shaken and mountains plunge into the depths of the sea. **R.**
There is a stream whose runlets gladden the city of God, the holy dwelling of the Most High. God is in its midst; it shall not be disturbed; God will help it at the break of dawn. **R.**

The LORD of hosts is with us; our stronghold is the God of Jacob. Come! Behold the deeds of the LORD, the astounding things he has wrought on earth. **R.**

Second Reading: 1 Corinthians 3:9c-11, 16-17

Brothers and sisters: You are God's building. According to the grace of God given to me, like a wise master builder I laid a foundation, and another is building upon it. But each one must be careful how he builds upon it, for no one can lay a foundation other than the one that is there, namely, Jesus Christ. Do you not know that you are the temple of God, and that the Spirit of God dwells in you? If anyone destroys God's temple, God will destroy that person; for the temple of God, which you are, is holy.

Alleluia: 2 Chronicles 7:16

R. Alleluia, alleluia.

I have chosen and consecrated this house, says the Lord, that my name may be there forever. **R.**

Gospel: John 2:13-22

Since the Passover of the Jews was near, Jesus went up to Jerusalem. He found in the temple area those who sold oxen, sheep, and doves, as well as the money-changers seated there. He made a whip out of cords and drove them all out of the temple area, with the sheep and oxen, and spilled the coins of the money-changers and overturned their tables, and to those who sold doves he said, "Take these out of here, and stop making my Father's house a marketplace." His disciples recalled the words of Scripture, *Zeal for your house will consume me.* At this the Jews answered and said to him, "What sign can you show us for doing this?" Jesus answered and said to them, "Destroy this temple and in three days I will raise it up." The Jews said, "This temple has been under construction for forty-six years, and you will raise it up in three days?" But he was speaking about the temple of his Body. Therefore, when he was raised from the dead, his disciples remembered that he had said this, and they came to believe the Scripture and the word Jesus had spoken.

SUNDAY, NOVEMBER 14
THIRTY-THIRD SUNDAY IN ORDINARY TIME
First Reading: Daniel 12:1-3

In those days, I Daniel, heard this word of the Lord: "At that time there shall arise Michael, the great prince, guardian of your people; it shall be a time unsurpassed in distress since nations began until that time. At that time your people shall escape, everyone who is found written in the book. "Many of those who sleep in the dust of the earth shall awake; some shall live forever, others shall be an everlasting horror and disgrace. "But the wise shall shine brightly like the splendor of the firmament, and those who lead the many to justice shall be like the stars forever."

Responsorial Psalm: Psalm 16:5, 8, 9-10, 11
R. (1) You are my inheritance, O Lord!
O LORD, my allotted portion and my cup, you it is who hold fast my lot. I set the LORD ever before me; with him at my right hand I shall not be disturbed. **R.**
Therefore my heart is glad and my soul rejoices, my body, too, abides in confidence; because you will not abandon my soul to the netherworld, nor will you suffer your faithful one to undergo corruption. **R.**
You will show me the path to life, fullness of joys in your presence, the delights at your right hand forever. **R.**

Second Reading: Hebrews 10:11-14, 18
Brothers and sisters: Every priest stands daily at his ministry, offering frequently those same sacrifices that can never take away sins. But this one offered one sacrifice for sins, and took his seat forever at the right hand of God; now he waits until his enemies are made his footstool. For by one

offering he has made perfect forever those who are being consecrated. Where there is forgiveness of these, there is no longer offering for sin.

Alleluia: Luke 21:36
R. Alleluia, alleluia.
Be vigilant at all times and pray that you have the strength to stand before the Son of Man. **R.**

Gospel: Mark 13:24-32
Jesus said to his disciples: "In those days after that tribulation the sun will be darkened, and the moon will not give its light, and the stars will be falling from the sky, and the powers in the heavens will be shaken. "And then they will see 'the Son of Man coming in the clouds' with great power and glory, and then he will send out the angels and gather his elect from the four winds, from the end of the earth to the end of the sky. "Learn a lesson from the fig tree. When its branch becomes tender and sprouts leaves, you know that summer is near. In the same way, when you see these things happening, know that he is near, at the gates. Amen, I say to you, this generation will not pass away until all these things have taken place. Heaven and earth will pass away, but my words will not pass away. "But of that day or

hour, no one knows, neither the angels in heaven, nor the Son, but only the Father."

SUNDAY, NOVEMBER 21
SOLEMNITY OF OUR LORD JESUS CHRIST, KING OF THE UNIVERSE

First Reading: Daniel 7:13-14

As the visions during the night continued, I saw one like a Son of man coming, on the clouds of heaven; when he reached the Ancient One and was presented before him, the one like a Son of man received dominion, glory, and kingship; all peoples, nations, and languages serve him. His dominion is an everlasting dominion that shall not be taken away, his kingship shall not be destroyed.

Responsorial Psalm: Psalm 93:1, 1-2, 5
R. (1a) The LORD is king; he is robed in majesty.
The LORD is king, in splendor robed; robed is the LORD and girt about with strength. **R.**
And he has made the world firm, not to be moved. Your throne stands firm from of old; from everlasting you are, O LORD. **R.**
Your decrees are worthy of trust indeed; holiness befits your house, O LORD, for length of days. **R.**

Second Reading: Revelations 1:5-8

Jesus Christ is the faithful witness, the firstborn of the dead and ruler of the kings of the earth. To him who loves us and has freed us from our sins by his blood, who has made us into a kingdom, priests for his God and Father, to him be glory and power forever and ever. Amen. Behold, he is coming amid the clouds, and every eye will see him, even those who pierced him. All the peoples of the earth will lament him. Yes. Amen. "I am the Alpha and the Omega," says the Lord God, "the one who is and who was and who is to come, the almighty."

Alleluia: Mark 11:9, 10

R. Alleluia, alleluia.

Blessed is he who comes in the name of the Lord! Blessed is the kingdom of our father David that is to come! **R.**

Gospel: John 18:33b-37

Pilate said to Jesus, "Are you the King of the Jews?" Jesus answered, "Do you say this on your own or have others told you about me?" Pilate answered, "I am not a Jew, am I? Your own nation and the chief priests handed you over to me. What have you done?" Jesus answered, "My kingdom does not belong to this world. If my kingdom did belong to this world, my attendants would be fighting to keep me from being handed over to the Jews. But as it is, my kingdom is not here." So, Pilate said to him, "Then you are a king?" Jesus answered, "You say I am a king. For this I was born and for this I came into the world, to testify to the truth. Everyone who belongs to the truth listens to my voice."

THURSDAY, NOVEMBER 25
THURSDAY OF THE THIRTY-FOURTH WEEK IN ORDINARY TIME OR THANKSGIVING DAY MASS

THURSDAY OF THE THIRTY-FOURTH WEEK IN ORDINARY TIME

First Reading: Daniel 6:12-28

Some men rushed into the upper chamber of Daniel's home and found him praying and pleading before his God. Then they went to remind the king about the prohibition: "Did you not decree, O king, that no one is to address a petition to god or man for thirty days, except to you, O king; otherwise he shall be cast into a den of lions?" The king answered them, "The decree is absolute, irrevocable under the Mede and Persian law." To this they replied, "Daniel, the Jewish exile, has paid no attention to you, O king, or to the decree you issued; three times a day he offers his prayer." The king was deeply grieved at this news and he made up his mind to save Daniel; he worked till sunset to rescue him. But these men insisted. They said, "Keep in mind, O king, that under the Mede and Persian law every royal prohibition or decree is irrevocable." So the king ordered Daniel to be brought and cast into the lions' den. To Daniel he said, "May your God, whom you serve so constantly, save you." To forestall any tampering, the king sealed with his own ring and the rings of the lords the stone that had been brought to block the opening of the den. Then the king returned to his palace for the night; he refused to eat and he dismissed the entertainers. Since sleep was impossible for him, the king rose very early the next morning and hastened to the lions' den. As he drew near, he cried out to Daniel sorrowfully, "O Daniel, servant of the living God, has the God whom you serve so constantly been able to save you from the lions?" Daniel answered the king: "O king, live forever! My God has sent his angel and closed the lions' mouths so that they have not hurt me. For I have been found innocent before him; neither to you have I done any harm, O king!" This gave the king great joy. At his order Daniel was removed from the den, unhurt because he trusted in his God. The king then ordered the men who had accused Daniel, along with their children and their wives, to be cast into the lions' den. Before they reached the bottom of the den, the lions overpowered them and crushed all their bones. Then King Darius wrote to the nations and peoples of every language, wherever they dwell on the earth: "All peace to you! I decree that throughout my royal domain the God of Daniel is to be reverenced and feared: "For he is the living God, enduring forever; his Kingdom shall not be destroyed, and his dominion shall be without end. He is a deliverer and savior, working signs and wonders in heaven and on earth, and he delivered Daniel from the lions' power."

Responsorial Psalm: Daniel 3:68, 69, 70, 71, 72, 73, 74
R. (59b) Give glory and eternal praise to him.
"Dew and rain, bless the Lord; praise and exalt him above all forever." **R.**
"Frost and chill, bless the Lord; praise and exalt him above all forever." **R.**
"Ice and snow, bless the Lord; praise and exalt him above all forever." **R.**
"Nights and days, bless the Lord; praise and exalt him above all forever." **R.**
"Light and darkness, bless the Lord; praise and exalt him above all forever." **R.**
"Lightnings and clouds, bless the Lord; praise and exalt him

above all forever." **R.**

"Let the earth bless the Lord, praise and exalt him above all forever." **R.**

Alleluia: Luke 21:28

R. Alleluia, alleluia.

Stand erect and raise your heads because your redemption is at hand. **R.**

Gospel: Luke 21:20-28

Jesus said to his disciples: "When you see Jerusalem surrounded by armies, know that its desolation is at hand. Then those in Judea must flee to the mountains. Let those within the city escape from it, and let those in the countryside not enter the city, for these days are the time of punishment when all the Scriptures are fulfilled. Woe to pregnant women and nursing mothers in those days, for a terrible calamity will come upon the earth and a wrathful judgment upon this people. They will fall by the edge of the sword and be taken as captives to all the Gentiles; and Jerusalem will be trampled underfoot by the Gentiles until the times of the Gentiles are fulfilled. "There will be signs in the sun, the moon, and the stars, and on earth nations will be in dismay, perplexed by the roaring of the sea and the waves. People will die of fright in anticipation of what is coming upon the world, for the powers of the heavens will be shaken. And then they will see the Son of Man coming in a cloud with power and great glory. But when these signs begin to happen, stand erect and raise your heads because your redemption is at hand."

THANKSGIVING DAY MASS
First Reading: Sirach 50:22-24

And now, bless the God of all, who has done wondrous things on earth; who fosters people's growth from their mother's womb, and fashions them according to his will! May he grant you joy of heart and may peace abide among you; May his goodness toward us endure in Israel to deliver us in our days.

Responsorial Psalm: Psalm 145:2-3, 4-5, 6-7, 8-9, 10-11
R. (1) I will praise your name for ever, Lord.

Every day will I bless you, and I will praise your name forever and ever. Great is the LORD and highly to be praised; his greatness is unsearchable. **R.**

Generation after generation praises your works and proclaims your might. They speak of the splendor of your glorious majesty and tell of your wondrous works. **R.**

They discourse of the power of your terrible deeds and declare your greatness. They publish the fame of your abundant goodness and joyfully sing of your justice. **R.**

The LORD is gracious and merciful, slow to anger and of great kindness. The LORD is good to all and compassionate toward all his works. **R.**

Let all your works give you thanks, O LORD, and let your faithful ones bless you. Let them discourse of the glory of your Kingdom and speak of your might. **R.**

Second Reading: 1 Corinthians 1:3-9

Brothers and sisters: Grace to you and peace from God our Father and the Lord Jesus Christ. I give thanks to my God always on your account for the grace of God bestowed on you in Christ Jesus, that in him you were enriched in every way, with all discourse and all knowledge, as the testimony to Christ was confirmed among you, so that you are not lacking in any spiritual gift as you wait for the revelation of our Lord Jesus Christ. He will keep you firm to the end, irreproachable on the day of our Lord Jesus Christ. God is faithful, and by him you were called to fellowship with his Son, Jesus Christ our Lord.

Alleluia: 1 Thessalonians 5:18

R. Alleluia, alleluia.

In all circumstances, give thanks, for this is the will of God for you in Christ Jesus. **R.**

Gospel: Luke 17:11-19

As Jesus continued his journey to Jerusalem, he traveled through Samaria and Galilee. As he was entering a village, ten persons with leprosy met him. They stood at a distance from him and raised their voices, saying, "Jesus, Master! Have pity on us!" And when he saw them, he said, "Go show yourselves to the priests." As they were going they were cleansed. And one of them, realizing he had been healed, returned, glorifying God in a loud voice; and he fell at the feet of Jesus and thanked him. He was a Samaritan. Jesus said in reply, "Ten were cleansed, were they not? Where are the other nine? Has none but this foreigner returned to give thanks to God?" Then he said to him, "Stand up and go; your faith has saved you."

SUNDAY, NOVEMBER 28

FIRST SUNDAY OF ADVENT

First Reading: Jeremiah 33:14-16

The days are coming, says the LORD, when I will fulfill the promise I made to the house of Israel and Judah. In those days, in that time, I will raise up for David a just shoot; he shall do what is right and just in the land. In those days Judah shall be safe and Jerusalem shall dwell secure; this is what they shall call her: "The LORD our justice."

Responsorial Psalm: Psalm 25:4-5, 8-9, 10, 14

R. (1b) To you, O Lord, I lift my soul.

Your ways, O LORD, make known to me; teach me your paths, Guide me in your truth and teach me, for you are God my savior, and for you I wait all the day. **R.**

Good and upright is the LORD; thus he shows sinners the way. He guides the humble to justice, and teaches the humble his way. **R.**

All the paths of the LORD are kindness and constancy toward those who keep his covenant and his decrees. The friendship of the LORD is with those who fear him, and his covenant, for their instruction. **R.**

Second Reading: 1 Thessalonians 3:12-4:2

Brothers and sisters: May the Lord make you increase and abound in love for one another and for all, just as we have for you, so as to strengthen your hearts, to be blameless in holiness before our God and Father at the coming of our Lord Jesus with all his holy ones. Amen. Finally, brothers and sisters, we earnestly ask and exhort you in the Lord Jesus that, as you received from us how you should conduct yourselves to please God and as you are conducting yourselves you do so even more. For you know what instructions we gave you through the Lord Jesus.

Alleluia: Psalm 85:8
R. Alleluia, alleluia.
Show us Lord, your love; and grant us your salvation. **R.**

Gospel: Luke 21:25-28, 34-36
Jesus said to his disciples: "There will be signs in the sun, the moon, and the stars, and on earth nations will be in dismay, perplexed by the roaring of the sea and the waves. People will die of fright in anticipation of what is coming upon the world, for the powers of the heavens will be shaken. And then they will see the Son of Man coming in a cloud with power and great glory. But when these signs begin to happen, stand erect and raise your heads because your

redemption is at hand. "Beware that your hearts do not become drowsy from carousing and drunkenness and the anxieties of daily life, and that day catch you by surprise like a trap. For that day will assault everyone who lives on the face of the earth. Be vigilant at all times and pray that you have the strength to escape the tribulations that are imminent and to stand before the Son of Man."

TUESDAY, NOVEMBER 30
FEAST OF SAINT ANDREW, APOSTLE
First Reading: Romans 10:9-18

Brothers and sisters: If you confess with your mouth that Jesus is Lord and believe in your heart that God raised him from the dead, you will be saved. For one believes with the heart and so is justified, and one confesses with the mouth and so is saved. The Scripture says, *No one who believes in him will be put to shame.* There is no distinction between Jew and Greek; the same Lord is Lord of all, enriching all who call upon him. *For everyone who calls on the name of the Lord will be saved.* But how can they call on him in whom they have not believed? And how can they believe in him of whom they have not heard? And how can they hear without someone to preach? And how can people preach unless they are sent? As it is written, *how beautiful are the feet of those who bring the good news!* But not everyone has heeded the good news; for Isaiah says, *Lord, who has believed what was heard from us?* Thus, faith comes from what is heard, and what is heard comes through the word of Christ. But I ask, did they not hear? Certainly, they did; for *their voice has gone forth to all the earth, and their words to the ends of the world.*

Responsorial Psalm: Psalm 19:8, 9, 10, 11

R. (10) The judgments of the Lord are true, and all of them are just.

Or:

R. (John 6:63) Your words, Lord, are Spirit and life.

The law of the LORD is perfect, refreshing the soul; the decree of the LORD is trustworthy, giving wisdom to the simple. **R.**

The precepts of the LORD are right, rejoicing the heart; the command of the LORD is clear, enlightening the eye. **R.**

The fear of the LORD is pure, enduring forever; the ordinances of the LORD are true, all of them just. **R.**

They are more precious than gold, than a heap of purest gold; Sweeter also than syrup or honey from the comb. **R.**

Alleluia: Matthew 4:19

R. Alleluia, alleluia.

Come after me, says the Lord, and I will make you fishers of men. **R**.

Gospel: Matthew 4:18-22

As Jesus was walking by the Sea of Galilee, he saw two brothers, Simon who is called Peter, and his brother Andrew, casting a net into the sea; they were fishermen. He said to them, "Come after me, and I will make you fishers of men." At once they left their nets and followed him. He walked along from there and saw two other brothers, James, the son of Zebedee, and his brother John. They were in a boat, with their father Zebedee, mending their nets. He called them, and immediately they left their boat and their father and followed him.

DECEMBER

SECOND SUNDAY OF ADVENT

First Reading: Baruch 5:1-9

Jerusalem, take off your robe of mourning and misery; put on the splendor of glory from God forever: wrapped in the cloak of justice from God, bear on your head the miter that displays the glory of the eternal name. For God will show all the earth your splendor: you will be named by God forever the peace of justice, the glory of God's worship. Up, Jerusalem! Stand upon the heights; look to the east and see your children gathered from the east and the west at the word of the Holy One, rejoicing that they are remembered by God. Led away on foot by their enemies they left you: but God will bring them back to you borne aloft in glory as on royal thrones. For God has commanded that every lofty mountain be made low, and that the age-old depths and gorges be filled to level ground, that Israel may advance secure in the glory of God. The forests and every fragrant kind of tree have overshadowed Israel at God's command; for God is leading Israel in joy by the light of his glory, with his mercy and justice for company.

Responsorial Psalm: Psalm 126:1-2, 2-3, 4-5, 6.

R. (3) The Lord has done great things for us; we are filled with joy.

When the LORD brought back the captives of Zion, we were like men dreaming. Then our mouth was filled with laughter, and our tongue with rejoicing. **R.**

Then they said among the nations, "The LORD has done great things for them." The LORD has done great things for us; we are glad indeed. **R.**

Restore our fortunes, O LORD, like the torrents in the southern desert. Those who sow in tears shall reap rejoicing. **R.**

Although they go forth weeping, carrying the seed to be sown, they shall come back rejoicing, carrying their sheaves. **R.**

Second Reading: Philippians 1:4-6, 8-11

Brothers and sisters: I pray always with joy in my every prayer for all of you, because of your partnership for the gospel from the first day until now. I am confident of this, that the one who began a good work in you will continue to complete it until the day of Christ Jesus. God is my witness, how I long for all of you with the affection of Christ Jesus. And this is my prayer: that your love may increase ever more and more in knowledge and every kind of perception, to discern what is of value, so that you may be pure and blameless for the day of Christ, filled with the fruit of righteousness that comes through Jesus Christ for the glory and praise of God.

Alleluia: Luke 3:4, 6

R. Alleluia, alleluia.

Prepare the way of the Lord, make straight his paths: All flesh shall see the salvation of God. **R.**

Gospel: Luke 3:1-6

In the fifteenth year of the reign of Tiberius Caesar, when Pontius Pilate was governor of Judea, and Herod was tetrarch of Galilee, and his brother Philip tetrarch of the region of Ituraea and Trachonitis, and Lysanias was tetrarch of Abilene, during the high priesthood of Annas and Caiaphas, the word of God came to John the son of Zechariah in the desert. John went throughout the whole region of the Jordan, proclaiming a baptism of repentance for the forgiveness of sins, as it is written in the book of the words of the prophet Isaiah: *A voice of one crying out in the desert: "Prepare the way of the Lord, make straight his paths. Every valley shall be filled and every mountain and hill shall be made low. The winding roads shall be made straight, and the rough ways made smooth, and all flesh shall see the salvation of God."*

WEDNESDAY, DECEMBER 8
SOLEMNITY OF THE IMMACULATE CONCEPTION OF THE BLESSED VIRGIN MARY

First Reading: Genesis 3:9-15, 20

After the man, Adam, had eaten of the tree, the LORD God called to the man and asked him, "Where are you?" He answered, "I heard you in the garden; but I was afraid, because I was naked, so I hid myself." Then he asked, "Who told you that you were naked? You have eaten, then, from the tree of which I had forbidden you to eat!" The man replied, "The woman whom you put here with me she gave me fruit from the tree, and so I ate it." The LORD God then asked the woman, "Why did you do such a thing?" The woman answered, "The serpent tricked me into it, so I ate it." Then the LORD God said to the serpent: "Because you have done this, you shall be banned from all the animals and from all the wild creatures; on your belly shall you crawl, and dirt shall you eat all the days of your life. I will put enmity between you and the woman, and between your offspring and hers; he will strike at your head, while you strike at his heel." The man called his wife Eve, because she became the mother of all the living.

Responsorial Psalm: Psalm 98:1, 2-3ab, 3cd-4

R. (1) Sing to the Lord a new song, for he has done marvelous deeds.

Sing to the LORD a new song, for he has done wondrous deeds; His right hand has won victory for him, his holy arm. **R.**

The LORD has made his salvation known: in the sight of the nations he has revealed his justice. He has remembered his kindness and his faithfulness toward the house of Israel. **R.**

All the ends of the earth have seen the salvation by our God. Sing joyfully to the LORD, all you lands; break into song; sing praise. **R.**

Second Reading: Ephesians 1:3-6, 11-12

Brothers and sisters: Blessed be the God and Father of our Lord Jesus Christ, who has blessed us in Christ with every spiritual blessing in the heavens, as he chose us in him, before the foundation of the world, to be holy and without blemish before him. In love he destined us for adoption to himself through Jesus Christ, in accord with the favor of his will, for the praise of the glory of his grace that he granted us

293

in the beloved. In him we were also chosen, destined in accord with the purpose of the One who accomplishes all things according to the intention of his will, so that we might exist for the praise of his glory, we who first hoped in Christ.

Alleluia: Luke 1:28
R. Alleluia, alleluia.
Hail, Mary, full of grace, the Lord is with you; blessed are you among women. **R.**

Gospel: Luke 1:26-38
The angel Gabriel was sent from God to a town of Galilee called Nazareth, to a virgin betrothed to a man named Joseph, of the house of David, and the virgin's name was Mary. And coming to her, he said, "Hail, full of grace! The Lord is with you." But she was greatly troubled at what was said and pondered what sort of greeting this might be. Then the angel said to her, "Do not be afraid, Mary, for you have found favor with God. Behold, you will conceive in your womb and bear a son, and you shall name him Jesus. He will be great and will be called Son of the Most High, and the Lord God will give him the throne of David his father, and he will rule over the house of Jacob forever, and of his Kingdom there will be no end." But Mary said to the angel,

"How can this be, since I have no relations with a man?" And the angel said to her in reply, "The Holy Spirit will come upon you, and the power of the Most High will overshadow you. Therefore, the child to be born will be called holy, the Son of God. And behold, Elizabeth, your relative, has also conceived a son in her old age, and this is the sixth month for her who was called barren; for nothing will be impossible for God." Mary said, "Behold, I am the handmaid of the Lord. May it be done to me according to your word." Then the angel departed from her.

SUNDAY, DECEMBER 12
THIRD SUNDAY OF ADVENT

First Reading: Zephaniah 3:14-18a

Shout for joy, O daughter Zion! Sing joyfully, O Israel! Be glad and exult with all your heart, O daughter Jerusalem! The LORD has removed the judgment against you he has turned away your enemies; the King of Israel, the LORD, is in your midst, you have no further misfortune to fear. On that day, it shall be said to Jerusalem: Fear not, O Zion, be not discouraged! The LORD, your God, is in your midst, a mighty savior; he will rejoice over you with gladness, and renew you in his love, he will sing joyfully because of you, as one sings at festivals.

Responsorial Psalm: Isaiah 12:2-3, 4, 5-6

R. (6) Cry out with joy and gladness: for among you is the great and Holy One of Israel.

God indeed is my savior; I am confident and unafraid. My strength and my courage is the LORD, and he has been my savior. With joy you will draw water at the fountain of salvation. **R.**

Give thanks to the LORD, acclaim his name; among the nations make known his deeds, proclaim how exalted is his name. **R.**

Sing praise to the LORD for his glorious achievement; let this be known throughout all the earth. Shout with exultation, O city of Zion, for great in your midst is the Holy One of Israel! **R.**

Second Reading: Philippians 4:4-7

Brothers and sisters: Rejoice in the Lord always. I shall say it again: rejoice! Your kindness should be known to all. The Lord is near. Have no anxiety at all, but in everything, by prayer and petition, with thanksgiving, make your requests known to God. Then the peace of God that surpasses all understanding will guard your hearts and minds in Christ Jesus.

Alleluia: Isaiah 61:1 (cited in Luke 4:18)

R. Alleluia, alleluia.

The Spirit of the Lord is upon me, because he has anointed me to bring glad tidings to the poor. **R.**

Gospel: Luke 3:10-18

The crowds asked John the Baptist, "What should we do?" He said to them in reply, "Whoever has two cloaks should share with the person who has none. And whoever has food should do likewise." Even tax collectors came to be baptized and they said to him, "Teacher, what should we do?" He answered them, "Stop collecting more than what is prescribed." Soldiers also asked him, "And what is it that we should do?" He told them, "Do not practice extortion, do not falsely accuse anyone, and be satisfied with your wages." Now the people were filled with expectation, and all were asking in their hearts whether John might be the Christ. John answered them all, saying, "I am baptizing you with water, but one mightier than I is coming. I am not worthy to loosen the thongs of his sandals. He will baptize you with the Holy Spirit and fire. His winnowing fan is in his hand to clear his threshing floor and to gather the wheat into his barn, but the chaff he will burn with unquenchable fire." Exhorting them in many other ways, he preached good news to the people.

SUNDAY, DECEMBER 19

FOURTH SUNDAY OF ADVENT

First Reading: Micah 5:1-4a

Thus, says the LORD: You, Bethlehem-Ephrathah too small to be among the clans of Judah, from you shall come forth for me one who is to be ruler in Israel; whose origin is from of old, from ancient times. Therefore, the Lord will give them up, until the time when she who is to give birth has borne, and the rest of his kindred shall return to the children of Israel. He shall stand firm and shepherd his flock by the strength of the LORD, in the majestic name of the LORD, his God; and they shall remain, for now his greatness shall reach to the ends of the earth; he shall be peace.

Responsorial Psalm: Psalm 80:2-3, 15-16, 18-19

R. (4) Lord, make us turn to you; let us see your face and we shall be saved.

O shepherd of Israel, hearken, from your throne upon the cherubim, shine forth. Rouse your power, and come to save us. **R.**

Once again, O LORD of hosts, look down from heaven, and see; take care of this vine, and protect what your right hand has planted the son of man whom you yourself made strong. **R.**

May your help be with the man of your right hand, with the son of man whom you yourself made strong. Then we will no more withdraw from you; give us new life, and we will call upon your name. **R.**

Second Reading: Hebrews 10:5-10

Brothers and sisters: When Christ came into the world, he said: "Sacrifice and offering you did not desire, but a body you prepared for me; in holocausts and sin offerings you took no delight. Then I said, 'As is written of me in the scroll, behold, I come to do your will, O God.' "First he says, "Sacrifices and offerings, holocausts and sin offerings, you neither desired nor delighted in." These are offered according to the law. Then he says, Behold, I come to do your will." He takes away the first to establish the second. By this "will," we have been consecrated through the offering of the body of Jesus Christ once for all.

Alleluia: Luke 1:38
R. Alleluia, alleluia.
Behold, I am the handmaid of the Lord. May it be done to me according to your word. **R.**

Gospel: Luke 1:39-45

Mary set out and traveled to the hill country in haste to a town of Judah, where she entered the house of Zechariah and greeted Elizabeth. When Elizabeth heard Mary's greeting, the infant leaped in her womb, and Elizabeth, filled with the Holy Spirit, cried out in a loud voice and said, "Blessed are you among women, and blessed is the fruit of your womb. And how does this happen to me, that the mother of my Lord should come to me? For at the moment the sound of your greeting reached my ears, the infant in my womb leaped for joy. Blessed are you who believed that what was spoken to you by the Lord would be fulfilled."

SATURDAY, DECEMBER 25
THE NATIVITY OF THE LORD (CHRISTMAS)
(Vigil Mass)
First Reading: Isaiah 62:1-5

For Zion's sake I will not be silent, for Jerusalem's sake I will not be quiet, until her vindication shines forth like the dawn and her victory like a burning torch. Nations shall behold your vindication, and all the kings your glory; you shall be called by a new name pronounced by the mouth of the LORD. You shall be a glorious crown in the hand of the LORD, a royal diadem held by your God. No more shall people call you "Forsaken," or your land "Desolate," but you shall be called "My Delight," and your land "Espoused." For the LORD delights in you and makes your land his spouse. As a young man marries a virgin, your Builder shall marry you; and as a bridegroom rejoices in his bride so shall your God rejoice in you.

Responsorial Psalm: Psalm 89:4-5, 16-17, 27, 29
R. (2a) For ever I will sing the goodness of the Lord.
I have made a covenant with my chosen one, I have sworn to David my servant: Forever will I confirm your posterity and establish your throne for all generations. **R.**
Blessed the people who know the joyful shout; in the light of your countenance, O LORD, they walk. At your name they rejoice all the day, and through your justice they are exalted. **R.**
He shall say of me, "You are my father, my God, the rock, my savior." Forever I will maintain my kindness toward him, and my covenant with him stands firm. **R.**

Second Reading: Acts 13:16-17, 22-25
When Paul reached Antioch in Pisidia and entered the synagogue, he stood up, motioned with his hand, and said, "Fellow Israelites and you others who are God-fearing, listen. The God of this people Israel chose our ancestors and

exalted the people during their sojourn in the land of Egypt. With uplifted arm he led them out of it. Then he removed Saul and raised up David as king; of him he testified, 'I have found David, son of Jesse, a man after my own heart; he will carry out my every wish.' From this man's descendants God, according to his promise, has brought to Israel a savior, Jesus. John heralded his coming by proclaiming a baptism of repentance to all the people of Israel; and as John was completing his course, he would say, 'What do you suppose that I am? I am not he. Behold, one is coming after me; I am not worthy to unfasten the sandals of his feet.'"

Alleluia
R. Alleluia, alleluia.
Tomorrow the wickedness of the earth will be destroyed: the Savior of the world will reign over us. **R.**

Gospel: Matthew 1:1-25 or 1:18-25
The book of the genealogy of Jesus Christ, the son of David, the son of Abraham. Abraham became the father of Isaac, Isaac the father of Jacob, Jacob the father of Judah and his brothers. Judah became the father of Perez and Zerah, whose mother was Tamar. Perez became the father of Hezron, Hezron the father of Ram, Ram the father of Amminadab.

Amminadab became the father of Nahshon, Nahshon the father of Salmon, Salmon the father of Boaz, whose mother was Rahab. Boaz became the father of Obed, whose mother was Ruth. Obed became the father of Jesse, Jesse the father of David the king. David became the father of Solomon, whose mother had been the wife of Uriah. Solomon became the father of Rehoboam, Rehoboam the father of Abijah, Abijah the father of Asaph. Asaph became the father of Jehoshaphat, Jehoshaphat the father of Joram, Joram the father of Uzziah. Uzziah became the father of Jotham, Jotham the father of Ahaz, Ahaz the father of Hezekiah. Hezekiah became the father of Manasseh, Manasseh the father of Amos, Amos the father of Josiah. Josiah became the father of Jechoniah and his brothers at the time of the Babylonian exile. After the Babylonian exile, Jechoniah became the father of Shealtiel, Shealtiel the father of Zerubbabel, Zerubbabel the father of Abiud. Abiud became the father of Eliakim, Eliakim the father of Azor, Azor the father of Zadok. Zadok became the father of Achim, Achim the father of Eliud, Eliud the father of Eleazar. Eleazar became the father of Matthan, Matthan the father of Jacob, Jacob the father of Joseph, the husband of Mary. Of her was born Jesus who is called the Christ. Thus, the total number of generations from Abraham to David is fourteen generations;

from David to the Babylonian exile, fourteen generations; from the Babylonian exile to the Christ, fourteen generations. Now this is how the birth of Jesus Christ came about. When his mother Mary was betrothed to Joseph, but before they lived together, she was found with child through the Holy Spirit. Joseph her husband, since he was a righteous man, yet unwilling to expose her to shame, decided to divorce her quietly. Such was his intention when, behold, the angel of the Lord appeared to him in a dream and said, "Joseph, son of David, do not be afraid to take Mary your wife into your home. For it is through the Holy Spirit that this child has been conceived in her. She will bear a son and you are to name him Jesus, because he will save his people from their sins." All this took place to fulfill what the Lord had said through the prophet: *Behold, the virgin shall conceive and bear a son, and they shall name him Emmanuel,* which means "God is with us." When Joseph awoke, he did as the angel of the Lord had commanded him and took his wife into his home. He had no relations with her until she bore a son, and he named him Jesus.

Or:

Matthew 1:18-25

Now this is how the birth of Jesus Christ came about. When his mother Mary was betrothed to Joseph, but before they lived together, she was found with child through the Holy Spirit. Joseph her husband, since he was a righteous man, yet unwilling to expose her to shame, decided to divorce her quietly. Such was his intention when, behold, the angel of the Lord appeared to him in a dream and said, "Joseph, son of David, do not be afraid to take Mary your wife into your home. For it is through the Holy Spirit that this child has been conceived in her. She will bear a son and you are to name him Jesus, because he will save his people from their sins." All this took place to fulfill what the Lord had said through the prophet: *Behold, the virgin shall conceive and bear a son, and they shall name him Emmanuel,* which means "God is with us." When Joseph awoke, he did as the angel of the Lord had commanded him and took his wife into his home. He had no relations with her until she bore a son, and he named him Jesus.

THE NATIVITY OF THE LORD (CHRISTMAS)
(Mass during the Night)
First Reading: Isaiah 9:1-6

The people who walked in darkness have seen a great light; upon those who dwelt in the land of gloom a light has shone. You have brought them abundant joy and great rejoicing, as they rejoice before you as at the harvest, as people make merry when dividing spoils. For the yoke that burdened them, the pole on their shoulder, and the rod of their taskmaster you have smashed, as on the day of Midian. For every boot that tramped in battle, every cloak rolled in blood, will be burned as fuel for flames. For a child is born to us, a son is given us; upon his shoulder dominion rests. They name him Wonder-Counselor, God-Hero, Father-Forever, Prince of Peace. His dominion is vast and forever peaceful, from David's throne, and over his kingdom, which he confirms and sustains by judgment and justice, both now and forever. The zeal of the LORD of hosts will do this!

Responsorial Psalm: Psalm 96: 1-2, 2-3, 11-12, 13
R. (Luke 2:11) Today is born our Savior, Christ the Lord.
Sing to the LORD a new song; sing to the LORD, all you lands. Sing to the LORD; bless his name. **R.**
Announce his salvation, day after day. Tell his glory among the nations; among all peoples, his wondrous deeds. **R.**
Let the heavens be glad and the earth rejoice; let the sea and what fills it resound; let the plains be joyful and all that is in them! Then shall all the trees of the forest exult. **R.**
They shall exult before the LORD, for he comes; for he

comes to rule the earth. He shall rule the world with justice and the peoples with his constancy. **R.**

Second Reading: Titus 2:11-14

Beloved: The grace of God has appeared, saving all and training us to reject godless ways and worldly desires and to live temperately, justly, and devoutly in this age, as we await the blessed hope, the appearance of the glory of our great God and savior Jesus Christ, who gave himself for us to deliver us from all lawlessness and to cleanse for himself a people as his own, eager to do what is good.

Alleluia: Luke 2:10-11

R. Alleluia, alleluia.

I proclaim to you good news of great joy: today a Savior is born for us, Christ the Lord. **R.**

Gospel: Luke 2:1-14

In those days a decree went out from Caesar Augustus that the whole world should be enrolled. This was the first enrollment, when Quirinius was governor of Syria. So, all went to be enrolled, each to his own town. And Joseph too went up from Galilee from the town of Nazareth to Judea, to the city of David that is called Bethlehem, because he was of the house and family of David, to be enrolled with Mary, his betrothed, who was with child. While they were there, the time came for her to have her child, and she gave birth to her firstborn son. She wrapped him in swaddling clothes and laid him in a manger, because there was no room for them in the inn. Now there were shepherds in that region living in the fields and keeping the night watch over their flock. The angel of the Lord appeared to them and the glory of the Lord shone around them, and they were struck with great fear. The angel said to them, "Do not be afraid; for behold, I proclaim to you good news of great joy that will be for all the people. For today in the city of David a savior has been born for you who is Christ and Lord. And this will be a sign for you: you will find an infant wrapped in swaddling clothes and lying in a manger." And suddenly there was a multitude of the heavenly host with the angel, praising God and saying: "Glory to God in the highest and on earth peace to those on whom his favor rests."

THE NATIVITY OF THE LORD (CHRISTMAS)
(Mass at Dawn)
First Reading: Isaiah 62:11-12
See, the LORD proclaims to the ends of the earth: say to daughter Zion, your savior comes! Here is his reward with

him, his recompense before him. They shall be called the holy people, the redeemed of the LORD, and you shall be called "Frequented," a city that is not forsaken.

Responsorial Psalm: Psalm 97:1, 6, 11-12

R. A light will shine on us this day: the Lord is born for us.
The LORD is king; let the earth rejoice; let the many isles be glad. The heavens proclaim his justice, and all peoples see his glory. **R.**
Light dawns for the just; and gladness, for the upright of heart. Be glad in the LORD, you just, and give thanks to his holy name. **R.**

Second Reading: Titus 3:4-7

Beloved: When the kindness and generous love of God our savior appeared, not because of any righteous deeds we had done but because of his mercy, He saved us through the bath of rebirth and renewal by the Holy Spirit, whom he richly poured out on us through Jesus Christ our savior, so that we might be justified by his grace and become heirs in hope of eternal life.

Alleluia: Luke 2:14

R. Alleluia, alleluia.

Glory to God in the highest, and on earth peace to those on whom his favor rests. **R.**

Gospel: Luke 2:15-20

When the angels went away from them to heaven, the shepherds said to one another, "Let us go, then, to Bethlehem to see this thing that has taken place, which the Lord has made known to us." So, they went in haste and found Mary and Joseph, and the infant lying in the manger. When they saw this, they made known the message that had been told them about this child. All who heard it were amazed by what had been told them by the shepherds. And Mary kept all these things, reflecting on them in her heart. Then the shepherds returned, glorifying and praising God for all they had heard and seen, just as it had been told to them.

THE NATIVITY OF THE LORD (CHRISTMAS)

(Mass during the Day)

First Reading: Isaiah 52:7-10

How beautiful upon the mountains are the feet of him who brings glad tidings, announcing peace, bearing good news, announcing salvation, and saying to Zion, "Your God is King!" Hark! Your sentinels raise a cry, together they shout for joy, for they see directly, before their eyes, the LORD restoring Zion. Break out together in song, O ruins of Jerusalem! For the LORD comforts his people, he redeems Jerusalem. The LORD has bared his holy arm in the sight of all the nations; all the ends of the earth will behold the salvation of our God.

Responsorial Psalm: Psalm 98:1, 2-3, 3-4, 5-6.
R. (3c) All the ends of the earth have seen the saving power of God.
Sing to the LORD a new song, for he has done wondrous deeds; his right hand has won victory for him, his holy arm. **R.**
The LORD has made his salvation known: in the sight of the nations he has revealed his justice. He has remembered his kindness and his faithfulness toward the house of Israel. **R.**
All the ends of the earth have seen the salvation by our God. Sing joyfully to the LORD, all you lands; break into song; sing praise. **R.**
Sing praise to the LORD with the harp, with the harp and melodious song. With trumpets and the sound of the horn sing joyfully before the King, the LORD. **R.**

Second Reading: Hebrews 1:1-6

Brothers and sisters: In times past, God spoke in partial and various ways to our ancestors through the prophets; in these last days, he has spoken to us through the Son, whom he made heir of all things and through whom he created the universe, who is the refulgence of his glory, the very imprint of his being, and who sustains all things by his mighty word. When he had accomplished purification from sins, he took his seat at the right hand of the Majesty on high, as far superior to the angels as the name he has inherited is more excellent than theirs. For to which of the angels did God ever say: *You are my son; this day I have begotten you?* Or again: *I will be a father to him, and he shall be a son to me?* And again, when he leads the firstborn into the world, he says: *Let all the angels of God worship him.*

Alleluia
R. Alleluia, alleluia.
A holy day has dawned upon us. Come, you nations, and adore the Lord. For today a great light has come upon the earth. **R.**

Gospel: John 1:1-18 or 1:1-5, 9-14
In the beginning was the Word, and the Word was with God, and the Word was God. He was in the beginning with

God. All things came to be through him, and without him nothing came to be. What came to be through him was life, and this life was the light of the human race; the light shines in the darkness, and the darkness has not overcome it. A man named John was sent from God. He came for testimony, to testify to the light, so that all might believe through him. He was not the light, but came to testify to the light. The true light, which enlightens everyone, was coming into the world. He was in the world, and the world came to be through him, but the world did not know him. He came to what was his own, but his own people did not accept him. But to those who did accept him he gave power to become children of God, to those who believe in his name, who were born not by natural generation nor by human choice nor by a man's decision but of God. And the Word became flesh and made his dwelling among us, and we saw his glory, the glory as of the Father's only Son, full of grace and truth. John testified to him and cried out, saying, "This was he of whom I said, 'The one who is coming after me ranks ahead of me because he existed before me.'" From his fullness we have all received, grace in place of grace, because while the law was given through Moses, grace and truth came through Jesus Christ. No one has ever seen God. The only Son, God, who is at the Father's side, has revealed him.

Or:

John 1:1-5, 9-14

In the beginning was the Word, and the Word was with God, and the Word was God. He was in the beginning with God. All things came to be through him, and without him nothing came to be. What came to be through him was life, and this life was the light of the human race; the light shines in the darkness, and the darkness has not overcome it. The true light, which enlightens everyone, was coming into the world. He was in the world, and the world came to be through him, but the world did not know him. He came to what was his own, but his own people did not accept him. But to those who did accept him he gave power to become children of God, to those who believe in his name, who were born not by natural generation nor by human choice nor by a man's decision but of God. And the Word became flesh and made his dwelling among us, and we saw his glory, the glory as of the Father's only Son, full of grace and truth.

SUNDAY, DECEMBER 26

FEAST OF THE HOLY FAMILY OF JESUS, MARY AND JOSEPH

First Reading: Sirach 3:2-6, 12-14 or 1 Samuel 1:20-22, 24-28

God sets a father in honor over his children; a mother's authority he confirms over her sons. Whoever honors his father atones for sins, and preserves himself from them. When he prays, he is heard; he stores up riches who reveres his mother. Whoever honors his father is gladdened by children, and, when he prays, is heard. Whoever reveres his father will live a long life; he who obeys his father brings comfort to his mother. My son, take care of your father when he is old; grieve him not as long as he lives. Even if his mind fails, be considerate of him; revile him not all the days of his life; kindness to a father will not be forgotten, firmly planted against the debt of your sins—a house raised in justice to you.

Or:

1 Samuel 1:20-22, 24-28

In those days Hannah conceived, and at the end of her term bore a son whom she called Samuel, since she had asked the LORD for him. The next time her husband Elkanah was going up with the rest of his household to offer the customary sacrifice to the LORD and to fulfill his vows, Hannah did not go, explaining to her husband, "Once the child is weaned, I will take him to appear before the LORD and to remain there forever; I will offer him as a perpetual nazirite." Once Samuel was weaned, Hannah brought him up with her, along with a three-year-old bull, an ephah of flour, and a skin of wine, and presented him at the temple of the LORD in Shiloh. After the boy's father had sacrificed the young bull, Hannah, his mother, approached Eli and said: "Pardon, my lord! As you live, my lord, I am the woman who stood near you here, praying to the LORD. I prayed for this child, and the LORD granted my request. Now I, in turn, give him to the LORD; as long as he lives, he shall be dedicated to the LORD." Hannah left Samuel there.

Responsorial Psalm: Psalm 128:1-2, 3, 4-5
R. (1) Blessed are those who fear the Lord and walk in his ways.

Blessed is everyone who fears the LORD, who walks in his ways! For you shall eat the fruit of your handiwork; blessed shall you be, and favored. **R.**

Your wife shall be like a fruitful vine in the recesses of your home; your children like olive plants around your table. **R.**

Behold, thus is the man blessed who fears the LORD. The

LORD bless you from Zion: may you see the prosperity of Jerusalem all the days of your life. **R.**

Or:

Psalm 84:2-3, 5-6, 9-10.

R. (5a) Blessed are they who dwell in your house, O Lord.

How lovely is your dwelling place, O LORD of hosts! My soul yearns and pines for the courts of the LORD. My heart and my flesh cry out for the living God. **R.**

Happy they who dwell in your house! Continually they praise you. Happy the men whose strength you are! Their hearts are set upon the pilgrimage. **R.**

O LORD of hosts, hear our prayer; hearken, O God of Jacob! O God, behold our shield, and look upon the face of your anointed. **R.**

Second Reading: Col 3:12-21 or 3:12-17 or 1 John 3:1-2, 21-24

Brothers and sisters: Put on, as God's chosen ones, holy and beloved, heartfelt compassion, kindness, humility, gentleness, and patience, bearing with one another and forgiving one another, if one has a grievance against another; as the Lord has forgiven you, so must you also do. And over all these put on love, that is, the bond of perfection. And let the peace of Christ control your hearts, the peace into which you were also called in one body. And be thankful. Let the word of Christ dwell in you richly, as in all wisdom you teach and admonish one another, singing psalms, hymns, and spiritual songs with gratitude in your hearts to God. And whatever you do, in word or in deed, do everything in the name of the Lord Jesus, giving thanks to God the Father through him. Wives, be subordinate to your husbands, as is proper in the Lord. Husbands, love your wives, and avoid any bitterness toward them. Children, obey your parents in everything, for this is pleasing to the Lord. Fathers, do not provoke your children, so they may not become discouraged.

Or:

Colossians 3:12-17

Brothers and sisters: Put on, as God's chosen ones, holy and beloved, heartfelt compassion, kindness, humility, gentleness, and patience, bearing with one another and forgiving one another, if one has a grievance against another; as the Lord has forgiven you, so must you also do. And over all these put on love, that is, the bond of perfection. And let the peace of Christ control your hearts, the peace into which you were also called in one body. And be thankful. Let the word of Christ dwell in you richly, as in all wisdom you teach and admonish one another, singing psalms, hymns, and spiritual songs with gratitude in your hearts to God. And whatever you do, in word or in deed, do everything in the name of the Lord Jesus, giving thanks to God the Father through him.

Or:

1 John 3:1-2, 21-24

Beloved: See what love the Father has bestowed on us that we may be called the children of God. And so we are. The reason the world does not know us is that it did not know him. Beloved, we are God's children now; what we shall be has not yet been revealed. We do know that when it is revealed we shall be like him, for we shall see him as he is. Beloved, if our hearts do not condemn us, we have confidence in God and receive from him whatever we ask, because we keep his commandments and do what pleases him. And his commandment is this: we should believe in the name of his Son, Jesus Christ, and love one another just as he commanded us. Those who keep his commandments remain in him, and he in them, and the way we know that he remains in us is from the Spirit he gave us.

Alleluia: Colossians 3:15a, 16a

R. Alleluia, alleluia.

Let the peace of Christ control your hearts; let the word of Christ dwell in you richly. **R.**

Or:

Acts 16:14b

R. Alleluia, alleluia.

Open our hearts, O Lord, to listen to the words of your Son. **R.**

Gospel: Luke 2:41-52

Each year Jesus' parents went to Jerusalem for the feast of Passover, and when he was twelve years old, they went up according to festival custom. After they had completed its days, as they were returning, the boy Jesus remained behind in Jerusalem, but his parents did not know it. Thinking that he was in the caravan, they journeyed for a day and looked for him among their relatives and acquaintances, but not finding him, they returned to Jerusalem to look for him. After three days they found him in the temple, sitting in the midst of the teachers, listening to them and asking them questions, and all who heard him were astounded at his understanding and his answers. When his parents saw him, they were astonished, and his mother said to him, "Son, why have you done this to us? Your father and I have been looking for you with great anxiety." And he said to them, "Why were you looking for me? Did you not know that I must be in my Father's house?" But they did not understand what he said to them. He went down with them and came to Nazareth, and was obedient to them; and his mother kept all these things in her heart. And Jesus advanced in wisdom and age and favor before God and man.

MONDAY, DECEMBER 27
FEAST OF SAINT JOHN, APOSTLE AND EVANGELIST
First Reading: 1 John 1:1-4

Beloved: What was from the beginning, what we have heard, what we have seen with our eyes, what we looked upon and touched with our hands concerns the Word of life— for the life was made visible; we have seen it and testify to it and proclaim to you the eternal life that was with the Father and was made visible to us— what we have seen and heard we proclaim now to you, so that you too may have fellowship with us; for our fellowship is with the Father and with his Son, Jesus Christ. We are writing this so that our joy may be complete.

Responsorial Psalm: Psalm 97:1-2, 5-6, 11-12

R. (12) Rejoice in the Lord, you just!

The LORD is king; let the earth rejoice; let the many isles be glad. Clouds and darkness are around him, justice and judgment are the foundation of his throne. **R.**

The mountains melt like wax before the LORD, before the LORD of all the earth. The heavens proclaim his justice, and all peoples see his glory. **R.**

Light dawns for the just; and gladness, for the upright of heart. Be glad in the LORD, you just, and give thanks to his holy name. **R.**

Alleluia

R. Alleluia, alleluia.

We praise you, O God, we acclaim you as Lord; the glorious company of Apostles praise you. **R.**

Gospel: John 20:1a and 2-8

On the first day of the week, Mary Magdalene ran and went to Simon Peter and to the other disciple whom Jesus loved, and told them, "They have taken the Lord from the tomb, and we do not know where they put him." So, Peter and the other disciple went out and came to the tomb. They both ran, but the other disciple ran faster than Peter and arrived at the tomb first; he bent down and saw the burial cloths there, but did not go in. When Simon Peter arrived after him, he went into the tomb and saw the burial cloths there, and the cloth that had covered his head, not with the burial cloths but rolled up in a separate place. Then the other disciple also went in, the one who had arrived at the tomb first, and he saw and believed.

TUESDAY, DECEMBER 28
FEAST OF THE HOLY INNOCENTS, MARTYRS
First Reading: 1 John 1:5—2:2

Beloved: This is the message that we have heard from Jesus Christ and proclaim to you: God is light, and in him there is no darkness at all. If we say, "We have fellowship with him," while we continue to walk in darkness, we lie and do not act in truth. But if we walk in the light as he is in the light, then we have fellowship with one another, and the Blood of his Son Jesus cleanses us from all sin. If we say, "We are without sin," we deceive ourselves, and the truth is not in us. If we acknowledge our sins, he is faithful and just and will forgive our sins and cleanse us from every wrongdoing. If we say, "We have not sinned," we make him a liar, and his word is not in us. My children, I am writing this to you so that you may not commit sin. But if anyone does sin, we have an Advocate with the Father, Jesus Christ the righteous one. He is expiation for our sins, and not for our sins only but for those of the whole world.

Responsorial Psalm: Psalm 124:2-3, 4-5, 7cd-8

R. (7) Our soul has been rescued like a bird from the fowler's snare.

Had not the LORD been with us— when men rose up against us, then would they have swallowed us alive, when their fury was inflamed against us. **R.**

Then would the waters have overwhelmed us; the torrent would have swept over us; over us then would have swept the raging waters. **R.**

Broken was the snare, and we were freed. Our help is in the name of the LORD, who made heaven and earth. **R.**

Alleluia

R. Alleluia, alleluia.

We praise you, O God, we acclaim you as Lord; the white-robed army of martyrs praise you. **R.**

Gospel: Matthew 2:13-18

When the magi had departed, behold, the angel of the Lord appeared to Joseph in a dream and said, "Rise, take the child and his mother, flee to Egypt, and stay there until I tell you. Herod is going to search for the child to destroy him." Joseph rose and took the child and his mother by night and departed for Egypt. He stayed there until the death of Herod, that what the Lord had said through the prophet might be fulfilled, *Out of Egypt I called my son.* When Herod realized that he had been deceived by the magi, he became furious. He ordered the massacre of all the boys in Bethlehem and its vicinity two years old and under, in accordance with the time he had ascertained from the magi. Then was fulfilled what had been said through Jeremiah the prophet: *A voice was heard in Ramah, sobbing and loud lamentation; Rachel weeping for her children, and she would not be consoled, since they were no more.*

Printed in Great Britain
by Amazon